Journeying with John

Available in the Journeying With Series

Journeying with Luke
Journeying with John

JOURNEYING WITH JOHN

Reflections on the Gospel

James Woodward, Paula Gooder
and Mark Pryce

WESTMINSTER
JOHN KNOX PRESS
LOUISVILLE · KENTUCKY

First published in Great Britain in 2014 as *Journeying with John: Hearing the Voices of John's Gospel in Years A, B, and C* by Society for Promoting Christian Knowledge.

Published in the United States of America in 2016 by
Westminster John Knox Press
100 Witherspoon Street
Louisville, KY 40202

16 17 18 19 20 21 22 23 24 25—10 9 8 7 6 5 4 3 2 1

Cover design by Eric Walljasper
Cover art: © Eric Walljasper
Typeset by Graphicraft Limited, Hong Kong

Library of Congress Cataloging-in-Publication Data
Names: Woodward, James, 1961- author.
Title: Journeying with John : reflections on the gospel / James Woodward, Paula Gooder, and Mark Pryce.
Description: Louisville, KY : Westminster John Knox Press, 2016. | Series: Journeying with series | Includes bibliographical references.
Identifiers: LCCN 2015040680 (print) | LCCN 2015042195 (ebook) | ISBN 9780664260637 (alk. paper) | ISBN 9781611646535 ()
Subjects: LCSH: Bible. John--Criticism, interpretation, etc. | Church year. | Common lectionary (1992).
Classification: LCC BS2615.52 .W66 2016 (print) | LCC BS2615.52 (ebook) | DDC 226.5/06--dc23
LC record available at http://lccn.loc.gov/2015040680

For Christopher Rowland,
beloved scholar and teacher

'I am not a God afar off, I am a brother and a friend;
within your bosoms I reside, and you reside in me'

from Blake's 'Jerusalem' (John 4.18–19)

Contents

————•◦•————

Preface: What is this book about?

The Revised Common Lectionary has established itself both in Anglican parishes and in other denominations as the framework within which the Bible is read on Sundays in public worship. It follows a three-year pattern, taking each of the Synoptic Gospels and reading substantial parts of them in the cycle of the liturgical year. During each of the years of Matthew, Mark and Luke, at times extensive use is also made of John.

All three authors have extensive experience of reading, preaching, leading, learning and teaching within this framework. We have worked in a variety of contexts: universities, theological colleges, parishes, chaplaincies and religious communities. We share a passion for theological learning that is collaborative, inclusive, intelligent and transformative. This shared concern brought us together across our participation in various aspects of the life of the Diocese of Birmingham in 2007, and we started a conversation about how best we might help individuals and groups understand and use the Gospels. We aspired to provide a short resource for Christians with busy and distracted lives in which the Gospel narrative might be explained, illuminated and interpreted for discipleship and service.

We hope that this book will enable the reader (alone or in groups) to enter into the shape of the Gospel; to enter imaginatively into its life, its concerns, its message, and in doing so to encounter afresh the story of Jesus 'the Word made flesh' (John 1.14). John's Gospel offers us a wonderful opportunity to attend to the Good News of Jesus Christ through the particular way the narrative opens up the truth and light of God's love for the reader and for discipleship. The process that shaped this text will be familiar to those readers who have used other volumes in this series.

Our text here has emerged out of shared study and reflection. We attended to the Bible text and examined how best to break open the character of the Gospel. We wanted to offer a mixture of information, interpretation and reflection on life experience in the light of faith. Paula provides an introduction to the biblical text; Mark was encouraged to use his imagination to offer creative writing on each of the themes; and James offers reflections in a range of styles. We have all been able to comment on and shape each other's contributions. We hope that the book will be used in whatever way might help the learning life of disciples and communities of faith. We expect that some of the material might be used as a base for study days and preparation for teaching and preaching.

A short volume like this can make no claim to comprehensiveness. The criteria of choice of seasons and texts were determined by our attention to the liturgical year. The contents have been shaped by our attempt to present some of the key characteristics of the Gospel of John through the seasons. There has been plenty to choose from!

The Introduction offers a concise exploration of the main characteristics and themes of John's Gospel. Paula helps us into the Gospel text through a discussion of the particular shape of the book, how the writer presents the narrative and offers us a very distinctive way of listening to the life, death and resurrection of Jesus, and the main theological themes of the Gospel. This Introduction is completed with a piece of poetry written by Mark Pryce, who invites us into an encounter with the Gospel through a reworking of the message of the Prologue to John's Gospel.

In the subsequent eight chapters a pattern is followed that picks up the major seasons in the cycle of the Church's liturgical year. First, Paula offers us material to expound the particular style of the Gospel. John's theology is then distilled in poetry and prose, with Mark offering us imaginative spiritual insights grounded in the Gospel messages. In the third section James offers some pastoral and practical theological reflections holding together faith and experience. At the end of each chapter we ask the reader to consider this material in the light of their own understanding and experience. These questions might form the basis of group conversation and study.

We have used as our guide the material generated by the Anglican Communion focused on the Mission of the Church. These 'marks of mission' stress the doing of mission. In offering some reflections for action, conversation and prayer we seek to support our readers in faithful action as a measure of our response and encounter with the gospel of Christ in this Gospel. The work done on this theology of mission helps us to see that the challenges facing us relate to the formation of Christian communities to be a people of mission. That is, we are learning to allow every dimension of church life to be shaped and directed by our identity as a sign, foretaste and instrument of God's reign in Christ.

Throughout the book we have aimed to be as clear and concise as possible in our communication and to wear our biblical scholarship lightly, so that the material is both accessible and stimulating. At the end of the book we offer some resources for further learning.

We hope you will find this book useful, building as it does on our volumes on the Gospels of Mark, Luke and Matthew. These books are intended to encourage you into further thought and action as we seek under God's guidance to follow Christ and proclaim the gospel. We hope that it gives you a glimpse of how much we have gained from our collaboration on this project. We acknowledge the generosity of the Revd John Fairbrother and the Trustees of Vaughan Park Anglican Retreat Centre in Auckland, New Zealand for the hospitality given to Mark, allowing him the space to write many of the poems in this book. We thank Ruth McCurry, our editor, for her trust and forbearance. We also thank all those people and communities that have enriched, informed and challenged our responses to the Gospel.

James Woodward
Paula Gooder
Mark Pryce

Introduction

Getting to know the Gospel of John

Exploring the text

Introduction

Of all the Gospels, John's probably receives the most mixed response. For many Christians John contains some of the most iconic and well-loved stories in all the Gospels: stories like that of the woman at the well or Mary's recognition of Jesus at the empty tomb seem to express deep truths that otherwise we find hard to put into words. On the other hand, within the Christian tradition John's Gospel has been regarded with great suspicion; it was the last of the Gospels to be received fully into the Canon of Scripture. This ambivalence towards John has been long-lasting and it is only really with the introduction of the Revised Common Lectionary that the Gospel has begun to be read liturgically, alongside the three Synoptic Gospels. Even then, it does not have its own year, but is used to plug perceived gaps in the other Gospels throughout the three years.

This ambivalent attitude towards the Gospel stretches back to the earliest Christian centuries; John was not widely used among the earliest Christian fathers. There were some, of course, who saw its worth, but many treated it with deep suspicion. This was because John's Gospel was very popular among a movement known as Valentinian Gnosticism; in fact the first commentary on the Gospel was written by a Valentinian Gnostic called Heracleon. Gnosticism is a catch-all term used by modern scholars to describe those in the ancient world who placed great emphasis on 'knowledge'. Gnosticism took many forms within a number of many different religious backgrounds (from

Judaism to Zoroastrianism), and Valentinian Gnosticism was a particularly influential form with Christianity. One of its key features was that it recognized a demiurge who created the material world, produced by Wisdom but separate from God. The themes of John's Gospel made it particularly attractive to Valentinian Gnostics, and their enthusiasm for it made other Christians highly suspicious of it. This suspicion was not limited to the Gospel alone: the other books perceived as making up the Johannine collection – 1, 2, 3 John and the book of Revelation – had an equally difficult journey and were only fully accepted alongside the rest of the New Testament writings in the fourth century AD.

A Johannine collection?

This brings us to the question of whether there is a 'Johannine collection'. The books of John's Gospel, 1, 2 and 3 John and Revelation have variously been considered as a collection since the second century – though a number of writers, such as Irenaeus and Tertullian, included only 1 John among the epistles and not the other two. It is not hard to see why these books were so often considered together. Not only were they all attributed (either in the text itself or in Christian tradition) to someone called John, they also contain a number of key overlapping themes, like love, the importance of bearing witness and the significance of the revelation of secrets.

The problem of the so-called 'Johannine collection', however, is that despite the overlapping themes there are key differences. These include aspects of the writing style – the language used is very different in the different works – and word usage. Probably one of the most striking things to note is that although the word 'lamb' is used in both John's Gospel and the book of Revelation as a description of Jesus, a different Greek word is used in each (*amnos* in John and *arnion* in Revelation). This presents an intriguing conundrum that suggests that while there is a connection between John's Gospel, 1, 2 and 3 John and

Revelation, the works did not have a single, consistent author. As a result, scholars have put forward the possibility that these works might have arisen not from a single hand but from a community which reflected on the key themes contained in them – love, light, revelation, hope – and wrote about them in different styles. In answer to the question about whether there is a Johannine collection, therefore, the answer is 'probably', though not one written or authored by just one person.

Who wrote the Gospel?

The great Johannine scholar Raymond Brown has helpfully drawn a distinction between the 'writer' and the 'author' of a piece of work. We are accustomed to eliding the two and assuming that the person from whom ideas emerge is the person who writes them down. In the ancient world this connection was probably far looser (although even today ghost writers produce a large number of books 'authored' by others). There is extensive evidence that in biblical times the 'author' of a text was not automatically its writer. The best New Testament example of this is Paul in Galatians; in 6.11 he observes: 'See what large letters I make when I am writing in my own hand!' It could be assumed from this that up to this point he has not actually been writing, and has begun to do so by way of conclusion to the letter.

The implication of this for the Johannine collection is that the questions of who lay behind the traditions in the Gospel, who wrote them down, and who was involved in shaping the Gospel into its final form may all lead to separate, different answers. These answers are not easy to provide, but this does not mean that we cannot ask the questions. We simply need to acknowledge in advance how hard it will be to come to a clear and satisfactory conclusion.

The beloved disciple

The place to begin is with the identity of the disciple whom Jesus loved. The importance of the 'beloved disciple' in John's

Gospel has long been recognized. From chapter 13 onwards this unnamed disciple grows in significance within the narrative (see 13.23; 19.26, 34–35; 20.2; 21.7, 20–24; with a possible additional mention in 18.15 where a disciple is called 'another disciple' but not named). Indeed, chapter 13 aside, the beloved disciple becomes most important around Jesus' death and resurrection.

A strong connection is often made between the beloved disciple and the writer of the Gospel. This is for good reason. John 21.24–25 reads:

> This is the disciple who is testifying to these things and has written them, and we know that his testimony is true. But there are also many other things that Jesus did; if every one of them were written down, I suppose that the world itself could not contain the books that would be written.

The disciple referred to is clearly the beloved disciple, who was mentioned in the previous verses in chapter 21. The problem here is that, as many people acknowledge, chapter 21 appears to be an appendix added on to the end of the Gospel. This has led some to argue that this disciple is only responsible for chapter 21, not for the rest of the Gospel. While this is possible, most scholars see this reference as giving us some clue about whose testimony is to be found throughout the whole Gospel.

So far so good! Unfortunately this is about as good as it gets. The rest of the evidence available is much less clear. The next task is to explore who the beloved disciple was, and here things begin to get complicated. This unnamed 'beloved' disciple has often been associated with John son of Zebedee; since John is not mentioned at all by name in the Gospel, this has caused the possibility to be raised that the person behind this Gospel was indeed John son of Zebedee, who for reasons of modesty decided to refer to himself obliquely. The main problem with this theory, almost by definition, is that because the beloved disciple isn't named it is impossible to know who he was.

A more substantial problem is that John son of Zebedee was, as we know from the other Gospels, from Galilee; but in John's Gospel there is much less mention of Galilee than elsewhere, the beloved disciple appears only in Jerusalem, and, if 18.15 is seen as a reference to him, he is known to the high priest. It is not easy to explain why a fisherman from Galilee would be so well known in Jerusalem (and in a way that Peter appears not to be). Another, less significant consideration is that John and James are called 'the sons of thunder' in the Synoptic Gospels (Mark 3.17), but the tone of John's Gospel is far from thunderous.

The uncertainty raised by the suggestion that the beloved disciple was John son of Zebedee has caused a large number of other candidates to be proposed, including Lazarus (since Jesus loved him), John Mark (a young man connected to the Jesus movement: see Acts 12.12 and possibly also Mark 14.51), Matthias, a blood brother of Jesus, Thomas, a minor disciple who remains unnamed, Mary Magdalene, John the Baptist, or someone else by the common name of John.

The reality is that it is almost impossible to be confident about the identity of the beloved disciple. Indeed, so difficult is it to be certain who he was that a number of scholars argue that the disciple is symbolic: loved by Jesus as Jesus was loved by his Father, and representing Jesus' attitude to all those who hear his voice and respond to his call. While this theory works for much of the Gospel, it does not adequately account for the explanation in 21.24 that this disciple is testifying to these things and has written them down, which implies that the beloved disciple is an actual person.

'John's Gospel'

As its name suggests, John's Gospel was accepted relatively early (mid to late second century AD) to be associated with someone called John. Irenaeus (c.130–c.202 AD), who claimed to have the tradition from Polycarp (c.69–c.155 AD), associated the fourth Gospel with 'John, the disciple of the Lord, who leaned on his breast' (*Against Heresies* 3.1.1): in other words, in one neat movement John, the beloved disciple and the author of the Gospel were all associated together. It is often noted, however, that Irenaeus may have been mistaken or confused here, since elsewhere he says that 'Papias was a hearer of John and companion of Polycarp' (*Against Heresies* 5.33.4). Eusebius (*c*.263–339) notes, however, that Papias, a bishop in the early second century, was clear that he had never heard John the apostle speak, but he had heard and knew John the Elder, a Christian leader from the late first century. In the context of this it is striking to note that 2 and 3 John both make reference to 'the elder', and some argue that this could in fact be John the Elder.

The uncertainty around the ascription of the Gospel to 'John' has led to it being called by some simply the 'Fourth Gospel', which avoids the complexities proposed by naming it. However, since the authorship of the other three Gospels is also far from assured this seems to be overcautious.

We are left, then, with two strands concerning the authorship of John's Gospel: first, that the Gospel itself attributes the testimony and some form of writing to the beloved disciple; and second, that Christian tradition associates this Gospel with someone called John.

The structure of John's Gospel

It may seem odd to turn to the question of the structure of John's Gospel before resolving the question of authorship, but there is a reason for this which will become clear. One of the striking differences between John's Gospel and the other three is that in Matthew, Mark and Luke the adult Jesus goes to Jerusalem only once, at the end of his ministry. In John's Gospel he goes three times (2.13; 6.4; 13.1), something that gave rise to the tradition that Jesus' ministry was three years in length. As is clear even from the verse numbers that describe his visits to Jerusalem, however, these three visits to Jerusalem do not provide the structure for the Gospel.

A common structure proposed for the Gospel looks like this:

1.1–18	The Prologue
1.19—12.50	The Book of Signs – public ministry of Jesus (more focus on narrative than discourse)
13.1—20.29	The Book of Glory – revelation of Glory (more focus on discourse than narrative)
20.30–31	Concluding Statement
21.1–25	The Epilogue

As its name suggests, the first half of John's Gospel is structured around a number of signs, seven in all, which are interspersed with lengthy discussions of key Johannine themes. These signs are:

1 Changing water into wine (2.1–11)
2 Healing the royal official's son in Capernaum (4.46–54)
3 Healing the paralysed man at Bethesda (5.1–18)
4 Feeding the 5,000 (6.5–14)
5 Jesus' walk on water (6.16–24)
6 Healing the man born blind (9.1–7)
7 The raising of Lazarus (11.1–45).

It is these seven signs that give structure to the first half of the Gospel.

The second half of the Gospel turns attention towards Jesus' imminent death but in a very different way from the other Gospels. In John Jesus' death is focused strongly around the theme of glory, and the revelation of that glory at the right time. Chapters 13–20 tell the story of the events that lead up to Jesus' death but are heavily interspersed with the 'farewell discourses', or what Jesus wants to say to his disciples before he departs. Before and after these two major sections is added a prologue (1.1–18, on which more below) and an epilogue (21.1–25, which contains the famous narrative of Jesus' charge to Peter to care for his lambs).

The reason why chapter 21 is considered to be an 'epilogue' and not a natural part of the Gospel proper is that chapter 20 ends with the kind of flourish that marks the conclusion of a book:

> Now Jesus did many other signs in the presence of his disciples, which are not written in this book. But these are written so that you may come to believe that Jesus is the Messiah, the Son of God, and that through believing you may have life in his name.

And the start of chapter 21 implies that it is something of an afterthought: 'After these things Jesus showed himself again to the disciples by the Sea of Tiberias; and he showed himself in this way.'

The structural problems of John's Gospel

Chapters 1 and 21 are not alone in being anomalous in the structure of John's Gospel. Other striking problems exist. The geography jumps about, for example, so that in chapter 5 Jesus is in Jerusalem, but chapter 6 begins: 'After this Jesus went to the other side of the Sea of Galilee, also called the Sea of Tiberias' (6.1). Going to the 'other side' of the Sea of Galilee from Jerusalem is a startlingly odd description. There are chronological oddities too, such as in chapter 14.31 where Jesus proposes that they rise and go on their way, but this is something that only happens three chapters later, at the beginning of chapter 18.

The biggest and most striking anomaly in the Gospel is the well-known and well-loved story of the woman caught in adultery (7.53—8.11). The story is written with a completely different style from the rest of John's Gospel: the words used are different, as is the sentence structure. Indeed, many scholars acknowledge that the writing style is much closer to Luke's style than to John's.

More importantly, this story is not included in the earliest and most reliable manuscripts of John's Gospel, and when it does appear it is located in a different place, either after 7.36

or at the very end of the Gospel. Other manuscripts have it not in John's Gospel but in Luke's, either at the end or following Luke 21.38. As a result of this, many modern English translations, while they include the story, put it in brackets to indicate its uncertain position within the Gospel.

What all these structural problems indicate is that the Gospel cannot have been written at a single sitting. It was edited and re-edited throughout its early life, with additional material inserted for various reasons. Thus, although the overall shape of the Gospel remains, parts of it were added to and expanded over a number of years. This suggests that the search for a single person named 'John' who wrote the Gospel might be futile. While there is clearly someone whose eyewitness account gave rise to some of the Gospel, it continued to be adapted and changed as time went by. Whichever person or people adapted the Gospel, however, they all held relatively similar views. This is why the possibility has been raised that we should not in fact be searching for a single author but for a community shaped around the insights and reflections of that person's eyewitness account about Jesus. Out of this community may have emerged not only the Gospel but also the epistles and Revelation, and this would explain both the similarities and the differences between these books.

The Johannine community

For many years, Johannine scholars have attempted to reconstruct the history of the 'Johannine community'. The idea lying behind this is that there are parts of John's Gospel that appear to describe a development or change in attitude towards Judaism. A common example given is the difference between John 5.15–16, where the Jews begin to persecute Jesus because he heals people on the Sabbath, and John 9.22, which states that the parents of the man born blind are afraid that they will be 'put out of the synagogue' if they acknowledge who Jesus is. Reading between the lines of this scholars such as J. Louis Martyn and Raymond Brown have argued that there must have been different phases in the history of the Johannine community (or the Community of the Beloved Disciple, as Brown called it). These phases, they believed, can be seen in different parts of the Gospel.

They pursued this theory by tracing a history of increasing animosity between the Johannine community and their Jewish neighbours, proposing that these different parts were written at specific times to reflect and speak into this animosity. The theory was predicated on increasing conflict between John's community and the surrounding Jewish community, and attempted to trace the writing of the Gospel in the light of this history.

This theory is now less widely accepted than it used to be. Too much had to be read into the text and the evidence overly interpreted in order to be confident about the results of such a reconstruction. There is simply not enough evidence to propose, for example, that chapter 5 was written before chapter 9 and at a time when there may have been conflict but the Christians had not yet been expelled from the synagogues. A key problem with the theory is that it proposed that John's community became almost entirely isolated from those around it in the first century. From this it is very difficult to suggest that the Gospel progressed swiftly from being written at the end of the first century for an isolated sectarian community to being widely accepted early in the second century (on dating see more below).

This does not mean that there was no Johannine community. That still remains the best explanation for authorship, as noted above. Nor does it mean that no conflict existed between John's community and their Jewish neighbours in the late first century. The reference in John 9.22 seems best understood against a backdrop in which some people were afraid of being expelled from the synagogue. What it does mean, however, is that extreme caution must be applied before proposing an extensive and elaborate reconstruction of the history of a community on the basis of a few verses within the Gospel.

Dating and the John fragment

This brings us to the question of the dating of John's Gospel. John has traditionally been regarded as the last Gospel to have been written. It seems to contain a number of extended reflections, which may well have emerged over time. These reflections, dwelling on the nature of Jesus and the conflict with the Jews, seem to point to a later, rather than an earlier, date for the final form of the Gospel. The conflict between the Jews and John's community suggested in the text would fit more obviously in a post-70 AD context (for more on this see below). Having said that, we can be almost certain that the Gospel was in its final form by the end of the first century, or very early in the second century at the latest. This is because of the discovery of the P^{52} fragment from an Egyptian papyrus, which has been dated to the early second century. There are also references to parts of John's Gospel in the Egerton Papyrus 2 which can be dated to the mid second century. It is clear, therefore, that John's Gospel had travelled to and was being used in Egypt very early in the second century.

From all this it seems likely that while John's Gospel took some time to reach its final form late in the first century, it then quickly spread and rose in popularity early in the second century and was influential in Egypt early in its life as a Gospel.

The Jews and John's Gospel

We have made mention already of the description of conflict with the Jews in John's Gospel, and this subject now needs to be picked up and explored further. One of the most uncomfortable features of John's Gospel is that, unlike the Synoptic Gospels, it appears to be the Jews as a whole who are in conflict with Jesus during his ministry, not small groups like the

Pharisees or Jewish authorities. This is significant because it was the Johannine movement blaming the Jews as a whole for Jesus' death, rather than just their leaders, that laid the foundations for some of the worst acts of anti-Semitism that occurred in Christian history.

Some scholars have attempted to argue that the Greek for 'Jews' in John's Gospel (*Hoi Ioudaioi*) might be more a geographic term than a religious one, and might be better translated as 'the Judeans'. This would mean that John's point about those opposed to Jesus was less overtly directed at the Jews. This has not, however, garnered widespread support. Much more likely is that the antagonistic references to 'the Jews' throughout John's Gospel emerge from a context in which John's community felt besieged and beleaguered. This did not amount to an invitation to all subsequent Christians to behave in a similar way, of course, but does acknowledge that heightened conflict can cause communities to react more strongly than would be reasonable in other contexts.

The context most often suggested for this heightened tension is the period following the fall of the Temple in Jerusalem in 70 AD. Scholars in the early twentieth century regularly talked about a 'parting of the ways' taking place between Judaism and Christianity in the decades that followed the fall of the Temple. It was believed that the Jewish leadership moved to a place called Jamnia (Yavneh in Hebrew), and while there published 18 Benedictions to be prayed every day alongside the Shema ('Hear, O Israel, the Lord your God the Lord is One'). The twelfth of these benedictions is a prayer against heretics and was seen as a catalyst for the conflict between Jews and Christians at the end of the first century. The theories about the history of the Johannine community slotted into this account of Jamnia and its opposition to Christianity.

As with the Johannine community, it is now recognized that the proposal of a council that opposed Christians is an overinterpretation of the evidence. Even if a council had met at Jamnia (something for which there is very little evidence), their major concern would not have been countering Christianity but attempting to redefine the nature of Judaism following the loss of the Temple. The twelfth benediction is not even about Christians, but about heretics in general. Scholars now acknowledge that a 'parting of the ways' in the late first century would have been much more subtle and less final than was previously thought.

Any conflict that existed between Jews and Christians in the first century would probably have been localized and not systematic. Nevertheless, if there was conflict between certain groups the most likely time for this conflict was the end of the first century, after the fall of the Temple, when those who previously worshipped in the Temple were forced to rethink what it meant, now, to worship God. As different groups worked out their own self-definition, conflict almost certainly erupted between them. We need to acknowledge, however, that frustratingly little is known about this period and that caution must be employed before major reconstructions of what might have happened are embarked upon.

John's Gospel alongside Matthew, Mark and Luke

Clement of Alexandria, an early church father writing in the late second century, observed that whereas Matthew, Mark and Luke wrote about the physical or bodily facts of Jesus, John wrote a 'spiritual gospel' (cited in Eusebius, *History of the Church* 6.14.7). This has had a great impact on how the four Gospels have been regarded through the centuries. Matthew, Mark and Luke have been seen as 'historical' and not 'theological'; John's Gospel has been seen as 'theological' and not 'historical'. Modern scholarship recognizes that this is a false distinction: there is plenty of theology in Matthew, Mark and Luke, and John may well be more 'historical' than has popularly been supposed. Most importantly, many scholars would now maintain that the differences between the Gospels are due to the fact that the sources used in John came to him through an entirely different route from those used in Matthew, Mark and Luke – who may all have relied on a single original source. In the feeding of the 5,000, for example, the overlap in vocabulary and detail between Matthew and Mark is 65 per cent; between Mark and John it is just 5 per cent.

The differences between the Gospels are worth noting. John contains a good number of stories that are not in the other Gospels. Stories like the wedding at Cana and the raising of Lazarus are unique to John. At the same time a vast number of stories and parables that appear in the Synoptic Gospels are simply missing from John's Gospel. Possibly most striking of all is the difference in location within the Gospel of the cleansing of the Temple: in John's Gospel it is an event at the start of Jesus' ministry, and in the other Gospels it comes almost at the end. Also important is the date of Jesus' death: in John this takes place before the Passover begins, but in the other Gospels Jesus dies after it has begun. The challenge of John's Gospel is to explore the discrepancies in turn and to decide on a case-by-case basis how historically reliable each one is perceived to be.

The humanity and divinity of Jesus in John's Gospel

There are many different themes in John's Gospel: themes such as light and darkness and good and evil; themes that stress the importance of belief and witness to what is seen and heard; themes that focus the attention on the coming 'hour' and its significance for Jesus. Glory, the Spirit and the 'I am' sayings all interweave to produce the rich and thought-provoking Gospel we have today. These themes will be explored in turn below in the relevant chapters, but one stands out as being so important to the Gospel that it needs considering here as well.

Ernst Käsemann famously observed that the Jesus of John's Gospel is nothing more than 'God striding over the earth'.

In other words, he believed that in John's Gospel Jesus is not presented as fully human, a view that has subsequently been disputed vigorously. Although Jesus is clearly divine in John's Gospel he is also clearly human: he is described as being exhausted in John 4 and weeps at Lazarus' death in John 11. Despite this, it is easy to see why Käsemann could argue this case; Jesus seems so in control throughout this Gospel that the reader might well wonder whether his divinity is more important than his humanity.

It is at this point that we need to remember the presence of the Prologue in John. While it is very difficult to discern precisely when the Prologue was written or indeed when it was included in the Gospel, the main thing to remember is that it is now a full part of the Gospel as it stands. As a result, it is impossible to read the rest of the Gospel without first reading the Prologue. This is important, as the Prologue contains many of the themes that are significant in the rest of the Gospel, such as light and darkness, belief, witness, comprehension, life and the world. Most important of all in the Prologue is the theme of the Word becoming flesh and dwelling in the midst of God's people. It is this that casts light not only on John's attitude to the humanity of Jesus but on how we are to read the Prologue. The Prologue, placed as it is at the start of the Gospel, is the lens through which we are to read the rest of the Gospel. It provides the readings, notes and theological guidance from which we can make sense of the rest.

It is impossible to argue that Jesus is portrayed either as not fully God or not fully human, because right at the start we see this settled clearly and poetically. As we read our way through the Gospel those majestic phrases from the Prologue ring loud and clear in our minds: 'The Word was God . . . the Word became flesh and dwelt among us.' The word, fully God and fully human, is the person we encounter in the pages of the Gospel and it is he to whom the author of the Gospel bears witness.

Imagining the text

This poem is a paraphrase of the Prologue to John's Gospel, telling the story of God's plan of salvation: how the Eternal Word, through whom all things are created, sets out on a journey from the Father, becoming human, and healing broken creation through his death and resurrection. Now, in baptism and Eucharist, and through the life of the Holy Spirit in the world, our lives and communities continue to be transformed and nourished by God's creative power.

This story of salvation through the self-giving love and action of God in Christ sets the tone for all Christian mission, and so we place the poem at the outset of the book. It could be read in Advent, Christmas or Epiphany services, or at any time when there is a focus on the salvation of God through the Incarnation of the Lord Jesus Christ.

In the beginning is Eternal Word,
Abiding in the presence of the living God;
Before all things – divine Life lives as One,
Delighting in the unity and peace of love.

Then through the Word all being forms,
The Word is seed and womb and spark and force,
Of each thing living root and source,
The channel and the chart of life.

The Word-Life lightens every child,
Every woman, every man;
The Word-Light lives within each soul
And shines in all the life God founds.

And like a lover, an adventurer,
The Word sets out to find homeland,
Make journey, voyage, pilgrimage to dwell
Among a people where the light shall shine.

Unwelcome, wounded, spurned, the one
Who comes is lifted up to love upon the tree,
For wayward and unseeing are the lives which flow
From one true Life poured out as Origin and End.

And yet unquenchable this love which flares
Like fire upon a forest floor;
A ceaseless flame that burns in offered wounds
To set the darkened hearts ablaze.

Grace after grace pours from this new dug well
Sunk deep into the split rock of a torn side,
Water rising up to feed and bathe God's children
In the cleansing and the feasting: our fullness of life.

1

Advent and Christmas
John's incarnational theology

Exploring the text

John 1.1–18 as poetry and prose

The Prologue of John is one of the most beautiful pieces of writing in the whole of the New Testament, and no carol service would be complete without the rolling lyricism. So iconic is it that many people can quote its opening verses from memory. In the Greek the language and vocabulary of parts of the Prologue are strikingly rhythmic and poetic, and this has led many people to suggest that it is derived from a hymn sung by the early Christians.

This is not to say that the Prologue in its current form is a hymn. One of its oddities is that the poetry is spliced with sections of prose, which raises the question of how the Prologue reached the form that it has. Some suggest that the Prologue is made of up of an early hymn adapted to the contemporary context of John's Gospel by the addition of prose elements about John the Baptist, elements that mean that John's Gospel effectively begins in the same place as Mark's Gospel does, with John's message of repentance. Others are of the opinion that the Prologue was written later by the Gospel author(s) in order to pick up the themes of the Gospel at its beginning, and deliberately mixed poetry with prose as a means of grabbing the reader's attention.

The crux of the argument lies in the use of 'the Word' (Logos) to describe Christ. The Prologue is the only place where 'Logos' is used to describe Christ. Some argue that this is an indication that the poem already existed and was adapted to fit on the front of John's Gospel, while others maintain that the Prologue is attempting to do something different at the start of the Gospel and hence it is natural for them to use a descriptor of Christ that is only picked up implicitly in what follows.

Whether the poem element of the Prologue was newly written for its context or borrows from an earlier poem, its lyrical nature is clear and there is a good argument for laying out the Prologue in poetic form to emphasize its rhythm and feel. The paraphrase below illustrates this well.

John's Prologue: 1.1–5, 10–12, 14, 16–18

¹In the beginning was the Word,
and the Word was with God,
and the Word was God.
²He was in the beginning with God.

³All things came into being through him,
and without him not one thing came into being.
What has come into being ⁴in him was life,
and the life was the light of all people.
⁵The light shines in the darkness,
and the darkness did not overcome it.

¹⁰He was in the world,
and the world came into being through him;
yet the world did not know him.
¹¹He came to what was his own,
and his own people did not accept him.
¹²But to all who received him,
he gave power to become children of God.

[14]And the Word became flesh
and lived among us,
and we have seen his glory,
the glory as of a father's only son,
full of grace and truth.
[16]From his fullness
we have all received,
grace upon grace.

[17]The Law was given through Moses;
grace and truth came through Jesus Christ.
[18]No one has ever seen God;
it is the only Son,
close to the Father's heart,
who has made God known.

Jesus as Word and Light

When we look at this paraphrase, the inner structure of the Prologue is easy to see.

- 1.1–5: The Word and his relationship both with God and with the world he created
- 1.6–8: John the Baptist's witness to the light
- 1.9–13: The world's response to the light
- 1.14–18: The world's response to the Word.

Laid out like this, it is easier to see the two interwoven themes in the Prologue: Jesus as Word and Jesus as Light, and the response to Light and Word by those he came to dwell among. It is striking to note that each is encountered by a different sense: light with the eye and word with the ear. Jesus, eternal Word and Light of the world, then, is to be encountered and responded to; the Prologue prepares the reader for the need for this encounter and response.

The images of Jesus the Word and the Light meet in the Wisdom tradition and it is probably this that stands behind the theology that we find so carefully woven together in this passage. The opening of John 1.1 is widely accepted to be an echo of Genesis 1.1 – 'In the beginning God created the heavens and the earth' – but it is an echo that comes to us through numerous other Old Testament passages: passages such as Proverbs 8.22–23, 'The LORD created me at the beginning of his work, the first of his acts of long ago. Ages ago I was set up, at the first, before the beginning of the earth'; and Psalm 33.6–7, 'By the word of the LORD the heavens were made, and all their host by the breath of his mouth. He gathered the waters of the sea as in a bottle; he put the deeps in storehouses.' The Prologue picks up this concept of wisdom, God's Word, being present at the start of all things and connects both in the person of Jesus Christ.

When one weaves Jesus the Word together with the theme of light (verses 4–5 and 7–9), then light's ability to 'enlighten' and bring wisdom shows us the relationship between these concepts. Jesus the Word and Jesus the Light is Jesus the Wisdom of God, who brings wisdom into the world.

This observation draws our attention to John 1.5, which talks how the darkness encounters the light. The King James Version translates this verse as 'the light shineth in darkness; and the darkness comprehended it not'; in the NRSV it reads instead, 'the light shines in the darkness, and the darkness did not overcome it'. There appears to be a rather big leap from 'comprehension' to 'overcoming'. What is interesting is that both translations are possible: the Greek verb *katalambano* can mean either 'to comprehend' or 'to overtake'. The connection is clear: comprehension involves overtaking with the mind.

The reason why most modern translations use the word 'overtake' is contained in John 12.35: 'Jesus said to them, "The light is with you for a little longer. Walk while you have the light, so that the darkness may not overtake you. If you walk in the darkness, you do not know where you are going."' The meaning here seems to point more obviously to 'overtake', and so by extension implies that overtake is the better translation in 1.5. However, the importance of wisdom and Jesus the Word and the Light bringing wisdom into the world suggests that, at least in 1.5, John might have chosen *katalambano* advisedly to mean both overtake and comprehend; in other words, he is pointing to the fact that darkness simply cannot grasp the light when it encounters it.

The primary theme of the Prologue, then, concerns the source of true wisdom. True wisdom, the Prologue suggests, is to be found in the person of Jesus Christ. Those who respond to the Light, who recognize and welcome the Word made flesh dwelling among us, are those in whom wisdom is to be found. John 1, then, in its poetic way, sets up many of the themes that recur many times through the Gospel; light, wisdom, witness, belief and glory are explored here and then returned to again and again as the Gospel unfolds. As with all poetry, the Prologue needs to be savoured and reflected upon if we, unlike the darkness, are to comprehend the light it reveals to us.

Imagining the text

John's Prologue bears witness to the truth about God revealed in Jesus Christ, who is the one through whom all things come into being, the Light who enlightens every person. John draws our attention to John the Baptist sent by God as the prophet who bears witness to the Light (1.6–9); his mission and ministry are an inspiration for all Christian disciples as they witness to the Light who shines in their own situations. We are called to look for the light in the darkness of a broken world, even within the dark places of our own selves, our families, churches and communities. This dramatic monologue celebrates the outpouring of God's grace through creation, incarnation and redemption – a story of which we are sent by God to be witnesses.

Bearing witness to the Light

Before the beginning,
before time began,
before space took shape,
before all things,
there was God.

And God is God from everlasting,
'I am who I am',
the God who was, and is, and is to come.
God is One, and God is Three:
God is Creator, God is Redeemer, God is Spirit,
and the Three are living in the perfect unity of Love.

From God's life together,
out of God's unity and love
springs forth more life –
for God is Source of all being, creating Word, sustaining Power,
God is Love spilling over into abundant community:
the life of space and time,
the life of sea and land and sky,
the life of sun and moon and stars,
the life of day and night, light and dark,
the life of myriad plants and trees and creatures,
the life of insects, fish, and birds and beasts,
the life of human beings made in God's image,
male and female, of every race and language,
each one unique, breathing the breath of God,
a universe teeming with the divine energy.

See how the life of God flows through the created world:
this world is beautiful, diverse, this world is full of plenty,
and all the living creatures are connected,
for this is the creation of God –
God who is One and God who is Three,
the Trinity of Love,
the dance of teeming joy, surprised delight.

Bearing God's image,
free to choose the pattern of God's own life for our living –
to live in love and harmony –
we are at liberty to turn away,
to disfigure, exploit, exclude,
and we reject the way of peace,
we rupture the connections of friendship and interdependency.

Yet God does not abandon creation,
God who is Source, and Maker, and Sustainer,
God sends the eternal Word
leaping to be God with us,
Word from before all time made flesh in time:
Jesus, Son of Mary,
clarifying Light in the unseeing darkness of fear.

The Light shows us the way of love,
revealing the path which tends always to the fuller life –
and the Light absorbs into himself the dark hostility and
    chaos of our lostness,
drawing home his creation on the Cross,
and through the broken flesh
enlightening a new creation
freed from the terrors of fear and hate,
released into love.

Through him breathes the Holy Spirit,
God alive within us and between us,
deep source beyond us,
spring of love and life for all who drink from her
and follow where she leads,
so as the Word is sent among us,
and as the Light has come among us,
and as the Spirit breathes upon us,
so we too are sent, bearers of light and life
in God's ever-flowing stream of love and peace,
into a creation being healed.

Reflecting on the text

'The Word was made flesh and dwelt among us' The Incarnation: radical and creative and true?

God is known in so far as he is loved.

Is Christianity true? As we look at the representations of Jesus offered in the Gospels, whose reconstructed picture can we trust? What is the meaning of the images and words that surround the Christian doctrine of the Incarnation? What does it mean to affirm that Jesus the man was and is God? Theologians have long argued over this and it presents particular difficulties as we look at the market place of faiths in our ever more secular towns and cities.

Let us begin with conviction firmly based in John's Gospel. Jesus is God living a human life from conception through death to the completeness of the resurrection. In Jesus we see in human terms the life of God. The relationship of Jesus to God is the 'enhumanizing' of the eternal mutual love between Father and Son. The way in which the life of Jesus was created and empowered by the Holy Spirit was the working out in the conditions of this world the love at the heart of God. The love of God creates, sustains and perfects all existence.

If this is true, then we might seek to enrich our discipleship as we think about the following areas in which our convictions about the Incarnation are transforming.

First, by entering into the human race God became kith and kin to every human soul, past, present and future. Every human being is a child of God and a sister or brother of God's Son, Jesus. We are all God's family by his initiative. This is pure grace. Faith, then, is the moment when we recognize that because of Jesus we are God's children, and respond with gratitude and joy. Baptism is a sacramental act in which we acknowledge and celebrate adoption by God and are incorporated into the community of faith.

Second, we learn that even in human nature God can be his essential self. This is good news because it has two implications for us as human beings. Whatever our technological cleverness, harsh experience might tempt us to despair of our moral and spiritual possibilities. But the reality of God as being one of us shows us that we can be true to our spiritual and moral character. This is true of all people as human beings. The gospel tells us that God has healing for all the diseases and distortions of our imprisoned selves. It teaches us that we should look for goodness and wisdom in all human beings, whoever and wherever they might be.

The other implication is that if God could be truly himself within the limitations of humanity, then the heart of what it means to be God cannot consist of such things as immortality or infallibility or cosmic power. The heart of God's being must be something we can share; and that is love which surrenders self and accepts limitation and suffering for the good of others. It is here that we must look for the true image of God.

Third, the particular historical circumstances of the Incarnation show us that God's concern is with the whole life of the world, and not just with some limited department called religion.

'For God so loved the world that he gave his only Son, so that everyone who believes in him may not perish but may have eternal life' (John 3.16). This is why God prepared a nation that had nothing corresponding to a Church. Israel believed that God's law was for every aspect of life and work, and that community sprang from living all life in covenant with him. When God, in Jesus, shared our human life it was in that setting that he did so.

Fourth, by Incarnation God enters into the whole range of human experience, including suffering, both mental and physical, and indeed death itself. God's eternal, divine relation to pain and evil is a mystery; but here we see him enduring them just as we have to endure them within our own limited horizons. This identification implies sympathy and empathy at its very profoundest. It does not solve the problem of evil, but it may help us to trust where we cannot understand.

This brings us to the fifth consideration: God's making himself vulnerable to us, and his response to the suffering we inflicted on him – and still do, through the sabotage of the possibilities of good in his world and our addictions to the perversions of evil. That response is the greeting of 'Peace'. Faith in the Incarnation assures us, in a way that the ambiguities of history never could, that nothing we can do to reject God or harm his purposes will lessen his loving will of forgiveness towards us. Ultimate judgement may well turn on whether pride of self-engrossment can accept that forgiveness; but the offer will be made.

Sixth, in the resurrection of the incarnate Son we catch a glimpse of God's possibilities for the material order. Today there is a renewed interest in the spiritual dimensions of life and in the interaction between body and spirit. Easter holds out the promise that where human life has been lived in partnership and openness with the divine will of love, transformation of that body is possible. Our bodies can be changed to share in the divine glory. Indeed, that principle might also be applied to the whole of creation. We must hold on to a vision of the possibility of the transformation of nature, both now and in that new world of which Easter was a foreshadowing.

'And the Word became flesh and lived among us, and we have seen his glory, the glory as of a father's only son, full of grace and truth' (John 1.14). Here is the heart of John's incarnational theology. This identification with us sets Christianity apart and presents a universal appeal to all souls. Let us share this good news with others. Let us acknowledge all humankind as God's children. Let us look for wisdom in the entire world. Let us look outwards into the world and see God present and active. Let us imitate God's vulnerability by our forgiveness and care for the poor and marginalized. Let our concern for creation embrace all the world, everything living within it, and the sheer fragile beauty of the environment. Let these be marks of our Christmas good news. Let this Incarnation take possession of our hearts and lives.

Action, conversation, questions, prayer

First mark of mission: *To proclaim the Good News of the kingdom.*

The first mark of mission, identified with personal evangelism, encapsulates what mission is really about, because it is based on Jesus' own summary of his mission (Matthew 4.17, Mark 1.14–15; Luke 4.18; 7.22; cf. John 3.14–17). This should be the key statement about everything we do in mission.

Action

Reflect on different ways in which you and your community proclaim the Good News of God's love. How do you bear witness to God's light shining in darkness?

Conversation and questions

- Maybe your church calls people to worship God by ringing joyful bells on Sunday? Perhaps you have a particular

part in the worship service which celebrates the God of
life?

• Maybe through your everyday work and relationships you
try to bring hope into gloomy situations of poverty, anger
or grief among colleagues and neighbours?

Prayer

Creating, redeeming, sustaining God,
thank you that you are with us in Jesus Christ,
present among us, renewing our world.
Lord, in the power of your Spirit,
help us to proclaim the good news of your love
in every aspect of the way we live our lives
as individuals and as community.
Amen.

2

Epiphany

Revealing glory: signs and wonders

Exploring the text

John's Gospel, like Mark's, has no birth narrative. For the most part the Prologue to John's Gospel fills this gap. As we noted in the previous chapter, the Prologue's theology is so profound that it provides a wealth of themes to reflect on, not only at Christmas but at other times of the year too. It is, nevertheless, interesting to note that Christmas season themes run through John's Gospel, even if they are not focused in a birth narrative.

One of these is a theme that we might recognize as being connected with epiphany: the revelation of God's glory in the world. On one level, the whole of John's Gospel revolves round the theme of the revelation and recognition of God's glory. As a result, it could be said to be at its heart an Epiphany Gospel – although, of course, John's Gospel associates these themes with a different time of the Church's year, since it is on the cross that Jesus' glory is finally revealed in all its fullness.

Glory is one of those words that is deeply familiar but very hard to define. It brings with it intimations of fire, of shining light and of splendour as well as of God's nature. In the Old Testament the Hebrew word normally translated as 'glory' is the *kabod*. When this word is used of human beings it means their reputation, or what we can know of them. This helps us to understand something about God's glory; when used of God the word also refers to what we can know of God, as opposed to that which remains transcendent and unknowable. In Old Testament tradition, when God was present – or about to be present – this presence was thought to be accompanied by natural phenomena such as wind and earthquakes, and particularly lightning and fire. Over time this type of light became so associated with God's glory that it became an accepted way of talking about God's glory shining all around (see Luke 2.9).

John's message of the revelation of God's glory, which reaches it culmination on the cross, has these twin themes wrapped around each other – the revelation of God's true nature and the shiny splendour of that nature. Of all writers, John would have been most aware of the heavy irony involved in claiming that God's splendour was fully revealed on the cross.

It is in the light of this strand that the signs in John's Gospel become crucially important. The first sign – the wedding at Cana – makes the connection with glory. John 2.11 is the verse that both identifies what Jesus has just done as a sign and notes that this reveals his glory. This gives us an insight into what John thought Jesus' miracles were all about. In the Synoptic Gospels Jesus' miracles are 'just' miracles; Matthew, Mark and Luke make no attempt to reflect on their significance. John, in calling them signs and observing that they reveal Jesus' glory, points strongly and clearly to how we are to understand them.

In John Jesus does not 'just' do miraculous deeds in John for the sake of it (I would argue that he doesn't do this in Matthew, Mark and Luke either, but they do not make this quite so clear). In John's Gospel Jesus' signs reveal his glory; in other words, they reveal his true nature. As so often in John, we are guided as to how we are to interpret what is going on. We see what Jesus does through the lens of understanding more about who he is. So underpinning all of them is the recognition that as the Word made flesh who was with God at creation, Jesus can do no other than continue in that role:

- Creating wine from water (2.1–11)
- Bringing back to wholeness the royal official's beloved son (4.46–54)
- Healing the man paralysed at Bethesda (5.1–18)
- Feeding 5,000 people when they were hungry (6.5–14)
- Walking on the waters of chaos – the waters that God defeated at creation (6.16–24)
- Bringing light to a blind man's eyes (9.1–7)
- Bringing to life a beloved friend who had died (11.1–45).

All these things reveal the true splendour of the divine nature of Jesus, the Word made flesh, and so reveal his glory in the world. They are what we might expect the Word who was there at creation to do.

At the same time they reveal something profound about the character of the Word made flesh. He is generous beyond all measure, making available vast quantities of best-quality wine (each water jar would have held around 80–120 litres) and enough food to produce 12 left-over baskets of bread. He is compassionate when responding to a father's grief at the loss of his son, and weeping for his own beloved friend; he is caring, speaking gently to people in need. John's miracles are far more than miraculous acts; they are windows into the very nature of who Jesus is. This is why they reveal his glory.

We cannot leave the signs, however, without pausing at Jesus' odd comment in 2.4: 'My hour has not yet come'. It seems strange for him to say this and then go on to perform the sign after all. It reveals an important theme in John, which returns later in the Gospel. In chapter 7, Jesus' brothers encourage him to go to Jerusalem for the feast of the Tabernacles; and Jesus rebuffs them, saying that his hour has not yet come, but then goes anyway. Again this seems an odd reaction and not easy to understand.

What it appears to point to is that Jesus is working to God's timetable, not a human timetable. The 'hour' is God's, not ours, and will be fulfilled when the moment is right. At the same time, various events can and do anticipate the fulfilment of the hour. The wedding at Cana, then, is an early glimpse of future glory – it gives us a sense of who Jesus really is, in advance of the ultimate moment on the cross when we see in entirety who he is and what he came to do.

Imagining the text

We may recognize the scene at Cana all too well. Despite the best efforts of the organizers, and costly generosity of the hosts, there is not enough: the wine is about to run out! We may often feel something similar in our lives. What more do we have to give? There is never enough! Or we may feel it in our churches. We have worked so long and so faithfully, but our energy is sagging. Where is the next generation? The Church is drying up!

This poem imagines the scene of the wedding; the key characters in the story speak about their fear of not having sufficient, of the good things running out, of the humiliation that threatens to mar all their good intentions. Jesus, who turns water into wine, does not speak explicitly, but his glory is to be glimpsed in the dismay, joy and surprise that the guests experience through his transformation of what seemed like a dire situation. This is the promise of our baptism and transformed life lived with God in Jesus.

Guests at a wedding in Cana

The steward of the feast
Among poor farmers and tradesmen
weddings are a village affair.
Everyone takes the day off to celebrate
and all good hosts lay on
a party never to be forgotten.

The happy couple
Imagine then the shame
of communal disappointment and scorn
trickling down the years:
'Ours was the wedding
when the wine ran out.'

Mary the mother of Jesus
I could see they were not wealthy,
though their guests were giving it some!
It's every parent's nightmare
not to provide enough.

I knew His inclination:
give all when the time is right.
I brought Him their anxiety
that everything would run out.

The servants
In the moment of exhaustion
the beautiful gift of water
from the generous well
we drew on, as He told us:
source of their surprise,
our secret to be shared.

The host
Have you ever felt, I ask you,
like a guest at your own party?
Not through someone stealing your show
or pushing you out of the limelight,
but through sheer joy and relief
at the whole event being better
than ever you imagined.

The other guests
What more is there to say?
The others have covered it all.
And anyway dear friends,
. . . we are nearly blotto.

The disciples
We will remember
this first sign He gave:
His gift of sheer abundance
in a shrinking world.

Into the simple water
we bring what hurts and fails.
The glory that He makes here
God's will, as in heaven.

Reflecting on the text

John 2.1–11: The power of new wine

In October 1999, plans for a state visit to France by the President of Iran had to be abandoned because of a dispute over wine at a banquet. Invoking Muslim law, the President declared not only that he could not drink wine but he could not sit at a table where wine was served. The French declared that a dinner without wine was inconceivable. Protocol demands that a state visit must include a state banquet – so the dinner was cancelled, and the visit downgraded from a 'state' visit to an 'official' visit.

The disagreement caused hardly a ripple in the turbulent waters of diplomacy, but it drew attention to the complex history of wine. Wine has acquired different meanings, over time and in different cultures. In Islam, the ban on alcohol was only imposed by Mohammad in the seventh century. He decreed that the faithful might be able to drink wine in Paradise, but they should abstain from it on earth.

For the French, wine is not a danger but a benefit; it is a beverage that for thousands of years has facilitated social relationships and the making of alliances, and is a necessary element of important occasions. The French and wine – unique tradition and relationship; for them wine is an expression of national identity.

Wine has a particular meaning in the New Testament, and especially in this second chapter of John. The story of the wedding in Cana is familiar. The wine runs out and Jesus rescues the host from embarrassment by conjuring up an additional supply of some 160 gallons. To my reckoning that is about 64 dozen bottles. It was, as this is meant to suggest, quite a party!

For John, a fastidious and subtle author, there is a further depth and meaning in the text. One of the clues to what John makes of the story is to be found in the detailed description of the six stone water pots. They are of the kind used for the Jewish rites of purification. We are to understand the contrast of the water, standing for the ceremonial religion of Judaism, being replaced with wine.

Wine has now replaced water – and it is the best wine, symbolizing the grace and truth that entered the world through Jesus Christ. It is this new wine symbolism that we must grasp, and in the grasping make it our own.

John 5.1–18

Thirty-eight years I have sat by this pool, a tired lame man, on the same smelly bed, watching the world walk by. I have seen a lot. I chose the spot, which is by the main gates and crowded with pedestrian traffic. I joined others who like myself are infirm and down on our luck or even out to make a penny or two for food. So here we are, gathered around the pool, waiting, waiting for a miracle, misery in love with our own company.

And I tell you, why don't you try waiting for 38 years – it is a long time and a lot of time to waste. Of course, over the years I have found much to fill my mind. I have often said to myself that my life would be better if I could walk, if I had not been afflicted with this sad palsy. Perhaps my life would have been much different – important, like all those who pass me by here and seem intent on their own affairs. I sometimes dream about what might have happened if my body had not been bent. I could have danced and enjoyed the revelry passing through these gates.

But there are, I suppose, advantages to my lameness. On my pallet by the gate I have been privileged to see the world pass before me. I know the costumes, even the latest fashions, of my world; the traders and merchants provide me with a never-ending show. The camel drivers bring me news and share their gossip and the coins they toss me keep me fed. Perhaps there is something to be said for a negative income bracket!

So, like many others, here I am, alternating between self-pity and contentment. These are the only moods I think I know: a simple but variable wardrobe rotated endlessly until they have become the rut that I sit in comfortably. And I sit by the pool, my energies and expectations drained away, bleached by the sun, having become a fixture on this particular scene.

Time standing still in one place. Think about it for a moment. Thirty-eight years, months, weeks, days, hours, minutes and seconds. This time stuff is my constant companion, one who bears striking resemblance to my impossible fixedness.

And then, that day, I was in for a surprise. The surprise was Jesus of Nazareth, a complete stranger. He was a new face at the gate, or at least a face that I'd never seen and did not know. I knew enough to call him 'Sir'; I tell you, a life underfoot in a busy marketplace has taught me to treat those who can kick with real respect. And do you know what happened? Jesus walked right over, not waiting for an invitation or solicitation. He just walked to the pallet, looked down and asked me, 'Do you really want to get well?'

What a strange question, I thought. Of course I want to get well, but there is no one to put me into the water. I heard myself droning on, each excuse more lame than the last, as I wondered about this question. 'Do you really want to get well?' There I am, more lame than 38 years in one place, unmoved and unmoving. And Jesus went straight to the heart of the matter and said to me, 'Get up.' He said, 'Take your pallet and walk.'

The excuses had to finish. I did not need anyone to do it for me; it had all been done. Get up, walk into the kingdom, embrace the salvation, celebrate redemption. These thoughts were pounding away in my heart.

So what happened? I got up and walked. I responded to a man I had never met and did not even know. I got up, and after 38 years the whole of my life was different. I won't tell you the rest of the story – you might want to imagine what happened to me next. That day I became committed. Committed for life, and I learned the lesson that first of all we have to stop making excuses and stand up.

Action, conversation, questions, prayer

Second mark of mission: *To teach, baptize and nurture new believers.*

Action
Reflect on the different ways in which you and your church community help others to find faith in Christ and to continue learning and growing as disciples.

Conversation and questions
- Perhaps you are involved in helping children and people of all ages to understand more about God's love and abiding presence in Jesus Christ?
- Are there fellow disciples for whom you have a particular ministry of encouragement and nurture?

Prayer

Creating, redeeming, sustaining God,
Thank you that you know us with a perfect knowledge
and love us with an endless love.
Thank you that you call us to know you and to love you,
and to share the story of your renewing power in human lives.
Lord, in the power of your Spirit,
give us confidence to people of light,
welcoming others into the freedom we find in you.
Amen.

3

Lent

Exploring the text

Discourses

John's Gospel differs from the other three Gospels in many ways, but in terms of style one of the most striking differences is the inclusion of what scholars call 'discourses', which are lengthy or formal discussions of a subject. Interestingly, a number of these discourses occur in readings set for the Lenten period, though some also occur in Ordinary Time and elsewhere.

Anyone who has sat and listened to the Johannine discourses might well agree that they are lengthy discussions of a subject, although in fact, one intriguing feature of the discourses is that they are not actually very formal. They meander from subject to subject, often looping back to reconsider ideas previously abandoned. As a result they can be very difficult to follow and can appear quite repetitive. Another feature is that many of them begin as conversations. The discourse with Nicodemus in chapter 3 is an interesting case in point. It starts out as a dialogue between Jesus and Nicodemus, but after verse 9 Nicodemus does not speak again; all the English translations drop the speech marks halfway through the passage (though at different places in different versions), as it becomes clear that it is now a monologue and no longer a conversation.

This feature has inevitably caused scholars to question the historicity of the discourses and to postulate that instead they reveal the considered reflections of the author/community over time. However, it is worth noting that it is notoriously difficult to decide where Jesus' words end and the reflections take over. This suggests that a simple choice between 'historical' and 'non-historical' is a false dichotomy here. John's Gospel presents to us a different category of reflective historical memory: a memory that begins very firmly in history but has become so internalized that it becomes impossible to decide where history and reflection divide.

The discourses cover a wide range of subjects and contexts, and are so thoroughly woven throughout the Gospel that it is almost impossible to note where they begin and end. Some discourses take the form of a friendly conversation, as with Nicodemus (3.1–21) or the Samaritan woman (4.1–26); some arise out of conflict and disagreement, for example with the Jews, and often focusing on the nature of Jesus' authority (5.17–47; 7.15–44); some seek to address the confusion of the crowd, as in understanding the nature of the bread of life Jesus offers (6.22–60); and others still are addressed to the disciples, the most famous of all being the farewell discourse in John 14—17).

The central feature of the discourses is that each introduces a key theological category by which to understand Jesus and his relationship with the world. It is intriguing to note that although the discourses are hard to follow, they introduce some of the most vivid metaphors in all the Gospels: being born again (or from above), living water, the bread of life, the good shepherd, and so on. These metaphors catch the imagination and prompt further reflection themselves.

Indeed, the presence of these metaphors raises the question of how we should read and engage with John's discourses. The problem is that if we divide them into convenient-sized chunks then their overall impact is diminished. It often strikes me that John's discourses are more experiential than logical and that they meander for a good reason. If you listen to a long section of one of the discourses (30–40 verses, for example), it is hard to prevent your mind wandering, and your thoughts tend to expand around what you are hearing. This is especially true in those passages that contain the vivid metaphors about Jesus Christ and what he came to do, which suggests that the style of the discourses is as important as their content. They are offering to the reader/hearer a reflective, imaginative way of engaging with the Jesus they portray.

In other words, it may be that the discourses are illustrating that there is more to 'understanding' than simple knowledge of facts or the ability to grasp detail. True comprehension of the life and character of Jesus can only be grasped through extensive reflection. If this is true, then John's Gospel not only represents a different way of engaging with the Jesus story itself, it provides us, the readers, with the tools for a different method of engagement too.

This seems most obvious in the longest discourse of all – Jesus' farewell to his disciples in chapters 14—17. This discourse reveals all the features so far identified for these passages: it meanders and is very hard to split down into a clear structure, contains vivid imagery, like Jesus as the vine, and invites the reader into its content to reflect more deeply on the nature of Christ and of his relationship to the world and to his disciples.

Those who have attempted to give the farewell discourse a structure split it into four major sections; although these sections clearly overlap with each other, and there is a lack of agreement about where each begins and ends.

- The first section explores the concept of departure and return and introduces the concept of the Paraclete (or comforter) who will comfort the disciples in Jesus' absence (14.1–31).
- The second section introduces the image of the vine and reflects on the nature of Jesus as life-giving source for the community (15.1–17).

- The third section returns to the theme of Jesus' departure and the role of the Paraclete (15.18—16.33).
- The fourth section, sometimes known as the high priestly prayer and paralleled with the Lord's Prayer in the Synoptic Gospels, contains five petitions from Jesus to God about his followers.

Although not easy to follow in detail, the farewell discourse achieves something important. As with many other discourses delivered just before death (such as Moses' final blessing in Deuteronomy 33 or David's final words in 1 Chronicles 28—29), it provides the opportunity to focus our attention on the key teaching that should be remembered. By repeating this in different ways over the four chapters, John's Gospel weaves a strong image of interconnectedness between God and Jesus, Jesus and his followers, and the Paraclete and those Jesus leaves behind. Indeed, the overall impact of these four chapters provides the sense of strong community grounded in Christ, the source of all life, and it is this overall impact that helps us to comprehend what is going on here.

The discourses in John, then, challenge us to read the text in a different, more reflective way, and in doing so we are invited into an experience of Jesus Christ as the ground of our being.

Imagining the text

One of the alluring themes in John's Gospel is the attention given to Jesus' conversations. Across Years A, B and C the lectionary offers us an opportunity to contemplate many of these encounters. Some of these are extended dialogues, such as those with Nicodemus and the Samaritan woman at the well; some are fleeting, such as the words spoken with the woman accused of adultery. The length of the coversationis one kind of significance to consider, but there is also the intensity and quality of the encounter, and the style of Jesus' responses.

John's picture of Jesus portrays a person of wisdom who gives vast amounts of time to those who are searching for understanding and for transformation. He is also someone of profound insight and compassion who comes close to the very heart of people and situations swiftly and unobtrusively, allowing others to come close to him, sometimes acting with a dramatic energy (when he floods Cana with the finest wine, cleanses the Temple, raises Lazarus), sometimes quietly listening (to those accusing the woman of adultery, to Martha and Mary). The giving of valuable time and profound attention to others is a dimension of 'loving service' in which the mission of Christians is characterized by the attitude and approach of Jesus himself: to offer individuals time and to make a serious engagement with their life-story or searching questions – to take them seriously as human beings in search of salvation.

This poem is a celebration of the service of Jesus to others using characters from John's Gospel. You will hear the voices of the disciples, the thousands of people he fed and healed, the people he rescued, such as Lazarus, Martha and Mary, and the hosts at Cana, the Samaritan woman at the well, Nicodemus, the woman accused of adultery – and the millions of people who have found in his stories a way into God's kingdom.

People with whom Jesus talked, talk about him

He is a washer of feet:
skills in massage and chiropody unsurpassed.
He is a feeder of hungry mouths:
capacity for mass catering truly miraculous.
He is a healer of sicknesses, a rescuer of impossible
  situations:

Lazarus and the embarrassed host would say that nothing is
  beyond him.
But what he did for us
was even more exquisite,
and entirely unrequired:
he took notice,
and looked into our eyes,
and drew us into conversation.
This too is love.

Asking for water, he shared his needs with us
as well as his gifts.
He spent his time as generously
as his blood, his breath.
He listened to questions and accusations
like the wind searching trees in a forest:
watch them dance to his grace.

We like to think
that even when silent,
drawing in the sand,
he was doing careful sums of kindness:
working out how the cost of anger, shame, recrimination
could be wiped away,
his self-giving submerged like a seed
in the earth of our searching.

Seeing now in his light,
words fly out of stories
to nest in our minds' branches:
like a dense bush at dusk
we are singing with understanding.

Reflecting on the text

Losing our pastoral heart?

This is a personal reflection on the importance of the pastoral as a mark of mission in our ministry.

I remember a few years back overhearing a clerical colleague respond to a parishioner's request to visit a non-churchgoing member of the parish: 'Visiting – parish visiting? That's old hat these days.'

The lay reader returned from a management of time course determined not to give people any longer than 45 minutes of pastoral conversation. The aspiration may be commendable but as we reflect on the discourses in John's Gospel we might want to think about the importance of conversation – unhurried and discursive and spontaneous. What is our relationship to time and how do we use it, or waste it, in the course of our discipleship?

The concept of putting a limit on our time, and the response that visiting should be for the sake of contact and connection, may fill us with concern, guilt, agreement or bemusement. Time is precious, and it is, of course, impossible to meet everyone's expectations. It reminded me of a hospital chaplain who could not leave the building until he had visited every bed on his rota of wards for that day. We may wonder whether the only need he was meeting was his own. A spacious and generous approach to time allows the opportunity for a deeper attention – a richer pastoral knowledge and wisdom about our spiritual lives.

All this raises important questions about the management of time, but there is also something else going on. We need to understand how we choose to exercise our discipleship, and what perspectives shape the choices we make. There is a danger that the Church might be losing its pastoral heart. Why is this? We have ceased to invest in our interest in those around us and the richness of their lived experience. We prefer paper to people, computers to conversations: we now seek to manage our parishes and chaplaincies rather than to pastor them.

We imagine that an organized parish is alive and ready to take risks, but the communities and individuals who are the subject of our strategies are all too often feeling ignored on a deeper level. We are retreating into a carefully planned irrelevance – absorbed by a bureaucracy that distracts us from the time-consuming task of interpersonal care. We are failing to engage with people for their own sake.

Our theology can be enriched if we open ourselves up to people, their work and values, their hopes and anxieties. We can do this only if we make a choice to listen: to attempt to connect beyond the safety zone of our inward-looking religious worlds. I am constantly amazed at people's preparedness to open up the spiritual fabric of their life, to talk theology, to ask questions, if they are paid individual attention and are given unhurried time. Some of these encounters may emerge from conducting occasional offices with care. The mother arranging a baptism is also a stressed accountant worried about her work and how this balances with the responsibilities of motherhood; she is a spiritual person wanting to know more about how prayer works. The grandparents at a baptism party are anxious about what kind of world their little ones will grow up in. After the funeral of a younger person, at a gathering in the pub, a stranger is kind enough to ask: 'Where has all that left your head, vicar? Do you fancy a pint?'

Beyond the meetings, the forms, and ministerial appraisal sessions, the Mission Action Plans, the proper concern about numbers and finance, the lists and tasks, are the countless opportunities to engage. A card, a phone call, an invitation for a drink, a visit – these are the lifeblood of hearts that can be recreated through a commitment to pastoral care.

If we believed that this task was important, then we would find time for it. I am not arguing for compulsive activity. Being over-busy (look how important I am) or tired (looking after others can be a substitute for caring for ourselves) is a characteristic of the clergy today. We hardly convey life in all its fullness because we cannot stand still long enough to look at it.

We are afraid of allowing the experience of others to change us. As Christians, we can learn from others – for example, artists. Artists go deep into themselves to create. Let others and their stories set our theological agendas, as we move inwards, and outwards, towards a different set of priorities for the gospel.

If this resonates with you, then the challenge must be shared with colleagues in the hierarchy – those who labour under the conviction that they oversee. In our ecclesiastical self-preoccupation, we need to look outwards. We need to give a higher priority to the occasional offices and the opportunities they give us to connect. Let those on the outside help us to understand our ministry with a greater sense of realism.

We also need to create time to meet people on their ground. When was the last time we accompanied a parishioner to the workplace, listening to the realities of the office, hospital, farm or factory? We should put ourselves where we can meet people; the pub, community hall and school playground all offer the chance to establish friendships. Let us see time spent with people not as administration-time wasted, but people-time wisely spent.

This might mean reordering our use of time to create space for a wider range of pastoral encounters. It might mean that we lead by example, so that others in our church community can have the courage to be pastoral – opening up much of what is a closed group to more challenging conversations about life and God.

We need to set ourselves a feasible target for visiting, and stick to it. Even one quality visit a week will transform the relationship with scores of people in a year. Don't forget that people love a phone call or a postcard, too.

All this needs to be put into the context of collaboration with the whole people of God, where we release the potential of others, as we work together for the common good – sharing the joyful task of pastoral care with lay people, allowing them set the agenda for care.

The many diocesan schemes to train lay people to work with the clergy in visiting and care are a great ministerial innovation. Too often, though, these schemes make clergy volunteer managers rather than pastors, because among the clergy there is a deep confusion about the priest's identity and pastoral task. One way through this is to recover the art of visiting, and so rediscover for ourselves that which is being lost: a pastoral heart.

Action, conversation, questions, prayer

Third mark of mission: *To respond to human need by loving service.*

Action

Reflect on the different ways in which you and your community respond to a variety of needs that cast shadows over our lives at the present time.

Conversation and questions

- Perhaps there are lunch clubs and other community groups sponsored by your church to support local people?
- Perhaps you are involved in fundraising and education work for charities supporting people in need nationally and internationally?

Prayer

Creating, redeeming, sustaining God,
We thank you that you have made us as you have:
soul and body, mind and heart.
We thank you that we are strong and also vulnerable:
for our energy and our weariness,
for our resilience and our need.
We thank you for one another:
for all the different ways in which we are your children.
Lord, in the power of your Spirit,
help us to foster the fullness of life which is your gift for all
   creatures.
Amen.

4

Passion and Holy Week

Exploring the text

What kind of Saviour?

Each of the Gospels brings its portrayal of Jesus to a climax with his death. Although the themes are different in each Gospel, it is important to pay close attention to the themes that come to the fore in the crucifixion accounts, since they tell us something significant about how the Gospel writers saw the whole of Jesus' life. One of the intriguing features of John's Gospel is that these themes, which have been building from the first chapter onwards, become implicit rather than explicit around Jesus' death. They are clearly still there but must be looked for carefully. Four key examples illustrate this point well.

The first, and best known, is Jesus as the Lamb of God. In chapter 1 John the Baptist proclaims Jesus to be the Lamb of God who takes away the sin of the world (1.29, 36). This theme then drops out of the Gospel and is never explicitly mentioned again. However, John's Gospel places Jesus' death a whole day earlier than in the Synoptic Gospels. In the Synoptic Gospels the last supper is the Passover meal and hence marks the start of Passover. In John's Gospel Jesus' death takes place on the day before Passover starts (John says this three times: 19.14, 31, 42), and at 12 noon: hence at the same time as the Passover lambs would be being slaughtered for the festival. No explicit connection is made here, but it is clear that we the readers are intended to notice the implicit point that

Jesus the Passover lamb dies at the same time as all the other Passover lambs.

Another example is the theme of Jesus' glory. Expectation is built throughout the Gospel that Jesus' glory will be revealed at his crucifixion. This is first indicated at the wedding at Cana and is picked up in chapter 17 in Jesus' farewell prayer; Jesus prays that his disciples will see his glory (and the implication is that it will be revealed fully at his death: 17.24). Again, no explicit mention is made of Jesus' glory on the cross, but we are clearly intended to recognize and reflect upon the ways in which Jesus' glory is revealed as he dies.

A third example is the reference to Jesus being 'lifted up'. This theme occurs three times in the Gospel. In 3.14, Jesus' lifting up is paralleled with Moses' lifting up of the snake in the wilderness; in 8.28, Jesus tells the Jews that once they have lifted him up they will realize that Jesus is 'he'; and in 12.32–34, Jesus says that when he is lifted up he will draw all people to him. Unusually, the author then points out the connection between what Jesus says here and his death ('He said this to indicate the kind of death he was to die': 12.33). It appears that this is so important a point that the author is unwilling to allow it to pass unnoticed. This emphasis on 'lifting up' (alongside the previous theme of glory) has the effect in John of blurring what we would normally separate out as the death, resurrection and ascension of Jesus. In the other Gospels Jesus' moments of glory are at the resurrection and Ascension. In John's Gospel the death itself becomes the moment of glory, which reaches its fulfilment in the resurrection.

A final example is Caiaphas' iconic and ironic statement about Jesus that it is better for one man to die for the people than for the whole nation to be destroyed (11.49–50). Again, there is no reference of this by the time we reach Jesus' death itself, but the foundation has been laid to indicate that we are to read Jesus' death as vicarious, on behalf of the whole nation.

What these four examples draw our attention to is that 'the Passion narrative' in John really runs from the very beginning of the whole Gospel. Everything before chapters 18 and 19 lays the foundations, sets the scene and prepares the reader to recognize what is going on in Jesus' death. John's Gospel shows us that there is very much more to Jesus' death than simply one man dying alone and in agony, and that we are to understand this as we read the account of Jesus' Passion.

One of the key elements that the Gospel sets up is that of paradox. In John, Jesus' death is profoundly paradoxical: his time of terrible suffering becomes his hour of glory. We have waited ever since the wedding at Cana. Jesus is also the passive 'Lamb' but he is in total control of his destiny. As a lamb he is 'handed over' to death by several different people. Indeed, this theme is far more important in John than at first glance in English translations. The Greek word *paradidomi* is translated in chapters 13—19 variously as 'betrayed', 'handed over' and 'gave up'. Once this becomes clear, its significance in John's narrative becomes obvious. Judas hands Jesus over to the Jewish authorities (John 13.11, 21; 18.2, 5); the Jewish leaders hand him over to Pilate (18.30, 35), and Pilate hands him over to be crucified (19.16). Jesus the 'passive Lamb' is passed from pillar to post by Judas, the Jewish leaders and Pilate, but he remains in absolute control throughout his trial and death. He wrong-foots Pilate in their discussion of power and truth, and ultimately, when the moment comes for him to die, hands over his own spirit (19.30; the NRSV translation 'gave up' also translates *paradidomi*).

As with so much else in the Gospel, John's Passion narrative requires deep thought and reflection. The Gospel provides us with the material for that reflection as it weaves the story of Jesus in chapters 1—17, but then leaves us, as we read chapters 18—19, to make our own connections, to reflect on paradoxes and to ask for ourselves the question, 'What kind of Saviour do we see hanging on the cross?'

Imagining the text

'Behold the man,' says Pilate to the crowds (John 19.5), showing them Jesus as a humiliating spectacle, with a torturous crown of thorns and dressed in a royal robe of purple stained with his own blood from floggings and beatings. What kind of man is this? What kind of king? What kind of Saviour?

Though the man Pilate shows to the crowd is horribly brutalized, the man John's Gospel shows us has his dignity and integrity intact. He is wounded for sure, but he has not retaliated.

The King brought to stand by the side of the Governor in his headquarters is the victim of military strength and the plaything of political power. The King shown to us in John's Gospel still speaks the truth, still holds his silence, still refrains from empty words and a desperate show of power. He remains true to the kingdom not of this world.

The Saviour, of whom the religious authorities and secular rulers and frenzied mob seem ignorant, is the man they see as the broken fool staggering under the weight of a cross. John's Gospel shows him as the one who is lifted up, bearing in his fragile body the full cost of a love that brings healing and peace.

What kind of saviour?

You taught us the power of true gesture.
Not games for the crowd with prisoners' lives,
nor masquerading innocence by washing hands;
formulaic delusions;
you strip away to the bare flesh
of brutal floggings.
You never destroy.

54

Casting aside outer garments
in your vest you take hold of the ordinary feet
and do the foul work
which repulses even those who benefit.
In this way you craft a new order,
engendering ethos.
You decline all masks.

Your way of authority
is to cross the treacherous strait
which cuts divinity from humankind
in the small boat of your body,
skin stretched across bone
lurching through a storm of pain.
You mend the breach.

And your final flourish
is gentle, with superb eye
to turn the grieving woman and the lonely man
towards one another,
speaking no recrimination
but making home.
Yours is the genuine word.

Such is your coup,
mighty Saviour.

Reflecting on the text

What kind of Saviour? A cross in the heart of God

Good Friday is not a day for the squeamish.

John narrates the events in short order: the trial before Pilate; the decision of the crowd; Jesus carrying the cross to Golgotha; the crucifixion itself; darkness covering the earth. The Gospel of John does not offer the gory details of the crucifixion, though John's first readers would have had no trouble imagining the nails being driven into the wrists and then the feet, the hours of bleeding and hunger, the slow asphyxiation as the lungs begin to close, the sweat and blood pouring off the condemned as the body temperature rises with every struggling breath. Crucifixion was more than a means of death; it was a weapon of terror, exactingly designed by the Romans to produce the greatest amount of lasting pain over the course of a slow and degrading death. An inscription is written above Jesus' head, written in three languages, Latin, Greek, and Hebrew, so the point will be lost on no one in cosmopolitan Jerusalem: the King of the Jews – a mockery, a final nail in the spirit, an embarrassment and humiliation, a king dying the death of a common criminal. The soldiers take his clothes and divide them. A handful of brave disciples, his mother among them, remain at the foot of the cross. A few final thirsty words end the drama – and then there is cold, dark death.

On Good Friday the Church asks us to take a good, hard look at the violence and meanness of the world and the bloodiness of the cross, and God on the cross. The account of Jesus' trial and crucifixion is commonly referred to as his Passion. Often we think of the Passion as the suffering and death of our Lord. And indeed in this Passion we see the cross in the heart of God, the suffering God who in Jesus Christ has become captive and broken-hearted: God's heart torn between the folly of human sin and frailty and God's unquenchable desire for his creation.

Good Friday is a story of individual sin, betrayal and abandonment: of the priests, of Pilate, the soldiers, the bloodthirsty crowds, of Peter, Judas, the other disciples, of you and me.

But Good Friday is bigger than the individual character of sin. It is the story of God's unending love for God's broken world, a broken world full of senseless evil and violence, a world where the good die young and the old grow lonely, a world of wars and cancer, of corruption and pollution, a world where so often there is little reason to hope or dream.

The word 'passion' is usually thought of in terms of God's suffering. But there is another way to think of passion, another use of the word that is connected to God's love. God's love is patient and kind and passionate. Love bears all things, believes all things, hopes all things, and endures all things, to the end. Love does not go gently into that good night. On Good Friday God's heart is torn between the passion of sin-induced suffering and the passion of grace-filled love.

On the cross Jesus refuses to give in to the meanness and arrogance that surround him. In the face of evil and despair the passion of his loving remains. To the cries for blood from the crowd he doesn't respond. Against the clubs and whips that beat him he refuses to fight back. To Peter he utters the command to lay down the sword. To the soldiers who have torn his body to shreds he offers forgiveness. To the thief he whispers the hope of paradise. To the grieving disciples and his broken-hearted mother he offers a few words of comfort. On the cross the Passion of Jesus' suffering is surpassed only by the passion of his love. Only the tenacity of God's loving is greater than the tenacity of humanity's sin. In the heart of God there is a cross . . . and on that cross God shows the fire of his love, a fire that the cold darkness of sin and death will never overcome.

Just before he bows his head and gives up his spirit, Jesus offers two final words: 'I thirst.' In these words, we see the whole of the Gospel of John. In John, Jesus is the one for whom we thirst. He is the one who turns water into wine at the wedding of Cana. He is the one who becomes the water of life for the Samaritan woman at the well. He heals the blind man by washing him in the pool at Jerusalem. He offers his very blood to quench the thirst of his disciples at the last supper. He is the living water that will never run out. And now, in his dying words, Jesus says, 'I thirst.' Throughout the Gospel, up until this point, the implication is that we – the disciples, the crowds, the politicians, the outcasts – are all thirsty for him. In his final words, Jesus turns the story around, and says that he is thirsty for us. In these two words, God is saying to those at the foot of the cross, to those same disciples in their grief and faithfulness, to the soldiers executing the torture of the state, to the chief priests protecting their political interests, to Pilate saving face, to you and me, to the whole of the cosmos, Jesus says, 'I thirst for you.' At the beginning of the Gospel he turns water into wine, suggesting that he is the good wine that will never run out. Now, at the end, the soldiers offer him sour wine as an act of mercy as water and blood mingle down his body. He drinks, yet Jesus' thirst is not for wine. His thirst is to do the will of the one who sent him, and that will is love. On the cross Jesus is the thirsty, unquenchable, passionate love of God for all of us.

This is the faithful one who lays down his life for his friends, the good shepherd who will never stop searching for the lost sheep, the living water of our baptism, and the one who will carry us through the stormy waters and deliver us to the far banks of the Jordan. Through the sweat and blood, the thorns and nails, the mockery and humiliation, the burning fire of God's love in Jesus Christ remains.

After tasting the sour wine, he says, 'It is finished.' All goes black, and darkness covers the whole earth. On Good Friday Jesus goes on ahead of us, into the dark and the cold of death, and there he makes a fire, a fire of Easter light, and he'll be there, waiting for us.

Action, conversation, questions, prayer

Fourth mark of mission: *To seek to transform unjust structures of society, to challenge violence of every kind and to pursue peace and reconciliation.*

Action

Reflect on the different ways in which you and your community bring change for the better in human relationships.

Conversation and questions

- Perhaps you are involved with a local network supporting homeless people, refugees, those caught up in debt, poverty, hurtful relationships or harmful patterns of life?
- Perhaps you support a campaign group which works for change towards justice nationally and internationally?

Prayer

Creating, redeeming, sustaining God,
you live in the perfect unity of love.
Thank you for the gift of life lived in relationship,
especially for the people you have given us in love, care and
    colleagueship,
for family, for friends, for those who rely on us.
Lord, in the power of your Spirit,
help us not to hide from the challenges that face us,
give us grace to change all that disfigures and distorts
what you would have us be as neighbours
living peaceably and justly one with another.
Amen.

5

Easter

Exploring the text

Who are you?

John's Gospel prepares its readers for Jesus' death from as early
as chapter 1, when John the Baptist proclaims Jesus to be the
'Lamb of God who takes away the sin of the world'. Indeed, as
we noticed in the previous chapter, the whole Gospel is focused
on bringing us to the point of being able to recognize and
reflect on the theological significance of Jesus' death. This does
not mean, however, that John is more of a Good Friday Gospel
than an Easter Gospel; John more than makes up for the focus
on Jesus' death in chapters 20—21.

Mark's Gospel has one account of the empty tomb and
nothing more. Matthew and Luke each have an empty tomb
experience (Matthew 28.1–8; Luke 24.1–9), an encounter
with the risen Jesus which proves his resurrection (Matthew
28.9–10; Luke 24.13–35), and a further encounter in which a
commissioning takes place (Matthew 28.16–20; Luke 24.36–53).
John's Gospel has multiple accounts of each type of resurrection experience:

- An empty tomb experience for both Mary Magdalene (John
  20.1–2), and Peter and the beloved disciple (20.3–10).
- An assurance of resurrection experience for Mary Magdalene
  (20.11–18) and for Thomas (20.24–31).
- An appearance with commissioning for all the disciples
  apart from Thomas (20.19–23) and for Peter at the lake-
  side (21).

John goes to great lengths to ensure that we are aware of the impact and significance of the fact that Jesus is risen from the dead, that he does appear to his nearest and dearest followers and then sends them outwards to proclaim the Good News and to care for his sheep. The Gospel may be one that prepares us fully for Jesus' death, but it spends a lot of time exploring his resurrection too. It is not an either/or Gospel, it is both/and: death and resurrection take centre stage.

Indeed, so critical is the resurrection to the Gospel that John goes to great lengths to ensure that readers recognize and under-stand three key features of the narrative. The first is that the tomb really was empty. In the other Gospels the evidence offered for the emptiness of the tomb is that the angels say so. In John's Gospel, Mary, Peter and the beloved disciple all witness to the tomb being empty. The importance of this is emphasized at the end of John 20, where it is stressed that this is a new tomb in which no one had been laid before. To us this might appear to be an insignificant detail, but in fact the opposite is true. Tombs at the time of Jesus could accommodate many different bodies. Each new body would be laid on a different shelf in the tomb. It is, therefore, crucial to John's argument here to under-stand that there were no other bodies in the tomb.

John is subtly but nevertheless clearly building his case for Jesus' resurrection. His was the only body in this tomb, Mary sees the stone rolled away and both the beloved disciple and Peter see that his body has gone. This much is the negative evidence that John offers for Jesus' resurrection. He then moves on to the positive evidence and presents two accounts of meet-ings with the risen Jesus. Both of these events – the encounters with Mary Magdalene and with Thomas – are rightly very popular stories. They resonate easily, since their major focus is their recognition of who Jesus is and what difference this makes to them.

Mary's recognition of Jesus comes from him calling her name. It is a rather beautiful worked example of Jesus' own comments on being the Good Shepherd in John 10.3, where the shepherd 'calls his own sheep by name and leads them out'. The factor that causes Mary to recognize Jesus is not seeing him, nor even talking to him (she does both of these things before realizing who he is), it is being called by name. The saying of her name by the person she has called 'Rabbouni' for so long is what transforms her and enables her to see for herself that the person she is speaking to is not a stranger but a beloved teacher and friend.

Although the story of Thomas is in one way completely different – the factor that changes him is the invitation to put his finger in the wounds in the hands and side of Jesus – in another way it bears a striking resemblance to Mary's story. Thomas has, through the Christian centuries, suffered from the epithet 'doubting Thomas', and as a result what is really going on in the story is obscured. This inaccuracy comes as much from English translations as it does from tradition. The NRSV still has Jesus say to Thomas, 'Do not doubt but believe.' What Jesus actually says is, 'Do not be unbelieving but believing.' This is a crucial difference. The problem is not that Thomas doubts, but that he doesn't believe the testimony of the other disciples.

As is so clear throughout John, bearing witness is a vital part of relationship with Jesus; the other half of that dynamic is the ability to believe testimony when it is offered. What John's Gospel recognizes, however, is that while believing testimony might be the goal, it is a hard one to achieve without personal relationship. We do not know whether Thomas does in fact put his fingers in Jesus' wounds – in the story the change in him simply happens when Jesus offers him the chance to do so. As with Mary, it is an invitation to and a reminder of the relationship that allows Thomas to move from being unbelieving to believing.

The positive evidence offered by John's Gospel for Jesus' resurrection recognizes that the ability to believe testimony is interwoven with relationship. Both Mary and Thomas need the reminder of relationship before they are able to believe. Now, as then, belief in the resurrection begins with a relationship with the one who rose from the dead.

Imagining the text

We offer four poems for the Easter season, all of which meditate on John's descriptions of encounters with the risen Christ in the Gospel (chapters 20 and 21). Each poem moves from the darkness of grief, confusion and rage, through a dawning sense of Christ's purposes and presence, through to the daylight in which there is good news to share. This first poem, below, traces Mary Magdelene's journey before daybreak to the empty tomb in the dark garden, her encounter with the man she mistakes as the gardener, and the fulfilment of her mission to announce the resurrection to her fellow apostles. Three further darkness, dawn, daylight poems follow in Chapter 6.

Mary Magdelene's darkness (20.1–18)

Night set a trap:
the cave of not finding you,
then my frantic tangled run
through the dark tunnel of expectations.

Dawn is an exchange:
your late starlight of lucid questions
in place of my unseeing rage;
your voice seeds understanding
in my heart's frozen ground.

The first day is not for holding
but for listening, sending, telling;
warm sun rises on the garden
as your absence is shared
into presence.

Reflecting on the text

John 20.11–18: Living in the light of the resurrection

John's account of the resurrection in these verses is one of the most vivid and poignant stories in the Bible. Mary, standing outside the tomb, is utterly disconsolate; not only because of the death of Jesus but because, having discovered the tomb empty, she thinks the body has been taken away. Then, in a dramatic moment of recognition, she sees Jesus, who says to her: 'Do not hold me, for I have not yet ascended to the Father; but go to my brethren and say to them, I am ascending to my Father and your Father, to my God and your God.'

This scene, though it was not part of the earliest iconography of the Church, became a favourite for painters of the Renaissance. Giotto, Orcagna and Titian, for example, depict Mary in a brightly coloured cloak kneeling on the ground with her arms outstretched trying to grasp hold of Jesus, who somewhat in the manner of a rugby player warding off a tackle resists the movement. It was Mary's attempt to physically touch and hold on to Jesus that appealed to their imagination. Hence the traditional title of this scene: *Noli me tangere.*

Outside the south wall of Magdalen College chapel in Oxford, a sculpture by David Wynn depicts the scene very differently. Mary, a slight, delicate figure, very unlike the haggard, raddled woman of artists like Donatello, is looking at and through Jesus at the moment of recognition. Jesus stands with both hands pointing heavenward, somewhat in the manner of a priest celebrating Mass. It's not the clinging that is emphasized but the recognition and Ascension. This is much closer to the intention of the evangelist.

Writers down the ages have speculated sometimes strangely on Mary's touching and the reply of Jesus. A range of explanations have been given, from the fact that his wounds were painful to the inappropriateness of touching his risen body. All miss the point. They neglect the importance of the word 'yet' in the following sentence: 'Do not hold me, for I have not yet ascended to the Father.' The implication is that the time will come when it will be appropriate to hold him. Jesus says at the Last Supper, 'I am coming back to you. In just a little while the world will not see me any more, but you will see me' (John 14.18–19). He says, 'I shall see you again and your heart will rejoice with a joy that no one can take from you' (John 16.22). Jesus has promised his permanent presence with his followers, a joy that no one can take from them. Mary is trying to hold on to the source of her joy, since she mistakes an appearance of the risen Jesus for his permanent presence with his disciples. Jesus, in telling her not to touch him, indicates that his permanent presence is not by way of appearance but through the gift of the Spirit, which comes only after he has ascended to the Father. Instead of trying to hold on to Jesus she is commanded to go and prepare his disciples for the coming of Jesus, when the Spirit will be given.

When we think of the Ascension, most Christians have in mind the version presented in Luke: a temporal sequence of death, resurrection, then 40 days later the Ascension, followed by the coming of the Holy Spirit. This is not John's way of looking at it. For him. going up to Jerusalem to die, the resurrection, the Ascension and the coming of the Spirit are all part of one movement to the Father, one act of divine glorification in which Jesus is glorified and the Father is glorified through him. To put it extremely, you could say that the resurrection appearances in John are something of an embarrassment in his theology: it is this total movement of Jesus to the Father that allows his Spirit to dwell in his followers and for them to know him as the eternal Word of God.

Yet also in the resurrection tradition is the story of an appearance to Mary Magdalene. In Matthew, Mary Magdalene and the other Mary, after discovering the tomb empty, encounter the risen Christ on their way to tell the disciples: 'And behold, Jesus met them and said "Hail". And they came out and took hold of his feet and worshipped him. And then Jesus said "Do not be afraid; go and tell my brethren to go to Galilee, and there they will see me"' (Matthew 28.10). Similarly, the longer ending of Mark says: 'Now when he rose early on the first day of week, he appeared first to Mary Magdalene, from whom he had cast seven demons. She went and told those who had been with him, as they mourned and wept.' John, aware of this tradition, develops it in accord with his own profound spiritual understanding. He wants to convey the point that it is not the appearance, not seeing Jesus, that really matters, but rather, through the Spirit, it is the coming to share in the same relationship with the Father that Jesus enjoys.

The risen Lord tells Mary, 'Go to my brethren and say to them . . .' They were not his physical, literal brothers, of course, but had become his brothers through their relationship to his heavenly Father. 'Go and say to them I am ascending to my Father and your Father, to my God and your God.' Some people emphasize the unique sonship of Christ in a way that leaves no point of contact with the rest of us. Others so stress the human family that all Christian content is lost. John's finely balanced affirmation differs from both these approaches. Jesus has come to take us into the same relationship with the heavenly Father that he eternally enjoys. His Father has become our Father, his God has become our God; we are his brothers and sisters in a new family constituted by the Holy Spirit.

The Christian community for whom John wrote have this in common. For them, too, the resurrection of Jesus would have seemed to belong to the past. No original eyewitnesses would still be alive. One of John's themes is that it is no disadvantage to be a Christian of a later generation. Jesus goes on to tell Thomas, 'Have you believed because you have seen me? Blessed are they who have not seen and yet believe.' Mary in this passage does not recognize Jesus by sight, she thinks him to be the gardener. It is when he calls her by name, Mary, that the moment of recognition occurs. Christians of succeeding generations cannot see Jesus, but they have the Church's memories of him; they have the Holy Spirit who takes those memories and speaks to us through them. They – we – have the same God who addresses us personally in and through these words. Earlier in John's Gospel we come across the words 'The sheep hear his voice as he calls by name those who belong to him' (John 10.3). God addresses us by name in the deep places of our heart, calling us to keep close to him through all the ups and downs of human existence.

Every line of John's Gospel is written up in the light of a fundamental conviction about the resurrection. For John, the life and death of Jesus constitute a triumphant move to the Father: an Ascension, a glorification, which makes possible his Spirit being with us and the mutual indwelling of God in us and we in him. This mutual indwelling, which is at the heart of John's understanding of the gospel, is profoundly spiritual, deeply mystical. But in John it is never separated from obedience to Christ's words. If we love God we will obey Christ's command. His command is that we love one another. If we love one another God himself will come and dwell within us and we will dwell in him. Through this mutual indwelling we will come to love him and obey Christ's command, and so on. And all the time it is the Holy Spirit who makes this possible.

For John, the tradition of the Church about the resurrection of Christ was authentic, securely grounded in history. But we were not eyewitnesses, and to be a believer we do not have to become ancient historians. We have the Church's memories of Christ, long pondered in the light of the resurrection; we have the Holy Spirit. To study the Scriptures ourselves, to allow the Holy Spirit to speak to us through them, to be open to God's direct address to us personally, to be willing to be obedient to Christ and bring all aspects of our lives under his purview and in his service: all this is to discover joy that no one can take away, a peace that nothing can destroy.

Action, conversation, questions, prayer

Action

Reflect on how you and your community are sharing in the task of ensuring that the ecology of the earth flourishes as God intends.

Conversation and questions

- Perhaps you are making real efforts to be wise in the way that resources are used, personally and in your community?
- Perhaps you are using the political and economic power you have to ensure a more just and careful treatment of the earth's resources?

Prayer

Creating, redeeming, sustaining God,
giver of life,
thank you for the wonder of your creation,
for its diversity and interdependence,
for the dignity we have as your creatures one with another.
Lord, in the light of your sacrificial love,
alert us to the needs of the planet we share,
teach us the wisdom we need to be faithful stewards of your
    world.
Amen.

6

The Easter season

Knowing, belonging, loving

Exploring the text

The nature of the Church

Just as there are two stories of the empty tomb, and two stories of the recognition of the risen Jesus, so also there are two stories of commissioning of disciples by the risen Jesus. The first is discussed in Chapter 7, since it also functions as John's account of the sending of the Spirit at Pentecost; the second (found in John 21), is so important that it warrants its own exploration here.

Chapter 21 functions as an epilogue to the Gospel. The end of chapter 20 apparently brings the Gospel to a halt, with an explanation of why 'these things' were written (so that you may believe). Chapter 21 opens in Galilee. This is something of a surprise. Chapter 20.19–23 contains the account of the sending of the Holy Spirit, including Jesus' commissioning of the disciples: 'As the Father has sent me, so I send you.' Why, then, have they gone home to do what they used to do, which would be fishing? This stands in great contrast to Luke's account of the sending of the Holy Spirit, which was the apparent beginning of a complete change in the life and behaviour of the disciples. There are a number of possible explanations for this. One of these is that the account is wrongly placed, and happens before the sending of the Holy Spirit; another is that John's and Luke's accounts of the sending of the Holy Spirit are not to be seen as the same event but two different complementary events. In John's Gospel itself the reason seems clear – as far as Peter is concerned, this second sending is crucially important. In it he is forgiven for his betrayal, and the nature of his commission ('feed my lambs') is made clear. For Peter at least, the two commissionings are a vital part of bringing him to the point of being able to move onwards.

Another important feature of the story is that it bears a slight resemblance to Luke 5.1–11, in which Peter (Simon), James and John are first called to follow Jesus. The differences are sufficient to indicate that this is not the same account misplaced; for example, in Luke Jesus is in the boat with them, while in John he is not; in Luke the nets almost break, in John they do not; in John they then eat a meal, in Luke they do not, and so on. But what is striking is that John's account is reminiscent of Luke's. In other words, the disciples have to go back to the beginning in order to be able to start again. They are called again, follow again and then are able to be sent by Jesus to do what he has called them to do. This return to the beginning is also signalled by the fact that Jesus calls Peter by the name he had when he first followed Jesus – Simon.

The miraculous catch of fish becomes an eighth sign in the Gospel. The previous seven fall into the first half of the Gospel; this additional sign comes at the end. As we noted in Chapter 2, the purpose of the signs in John's Gospel is to point to who Jesus really is – to reveal his glory. This sign points to who the disciples are called to be – in a way, to reveal *their* glory. At their first calling in Luke 5 they are called to fish for people; here they bring in an enormous haul of fish which, despite being so great, does not break their nets. This is surely a sign of what they are called to be. They are called to fish for people, and to achieve a haul that is beyond imagining, but which, despite this, does not exceed what they are able to cope with.

None of this can happen, however, until Peter's betrayal of Jesus is forgiven and he is healed. Many commentators have observed how important it is that Peter is given the opportunity to affirm his love for Jesus three times, as a way to counteract and counterbalance his threefold denial. Indeed, it is striking to notice what it is that Jesus does ask of him. We might expect a three-fold apology – 'I'm sorry, I'm very sorry, I'm very, very sorry' – but this is not what Jesus requires. Instead Peter is asked to affirm the positive rather than recall the negative. He has to state, and restate, his love for Jesus. Somewhat intriguingly, two different Greek words for 'love' are used in this exchange. Jesus asks if Peter loves him using the verb *agapao* and Peter responds using the word *phileo*; until the final exchange, when Jesus also uses *phileo*. There has been much discussion about the importance of this, and the general consensus is that in fact it has little theological significance. It could be that John uses the two words interchangeably for 'love', as he does throughout the Gospel, for no other reason than the need for variety.

A similar change can be observed in Jesus' command to Peter – 'Feed my lambs', 'Tend my sheep', 'Feed my sheep'. Again the change appears to be for variety's sake, but the command itself is crucially important – 'love', for Jesus, should not be solely an intellectual exercise; it has consequence. Love has no focus or purpose unless it finds expression in care for Jesus' flock. In this account Peter is commissioned again, as he is at the start of Jesus' ministry in Luke's Gospel. There the command to follow is accompanied with the call to fish for people; here the command to follow (21.19) is accompanied with the call to feed Jesus' flock.

John's resurrection extravaganza serves to remind us that the point of Jesus' rising from the dead is not the event alone but the resurrection's transformative power to draw us once more to Jesus Christ and to send us outwards once more to show our love for him in the world.

Imagining the text

As mentioned in Chapter 5, we offer four poems for the Easter season, meditating on John's descriptions of encounters with the risen Christ in chapters 20 and 21. Each poem moves from the darkness of grief, confusion and shame, disappointment and hopelessness, through a dawning sense of Christ's purposes and presence, to the daylight in which there is good news of new life to share. The poem in Chapter 5 traced Mary Magdelene's journey on Easter morning (20.1–18). The three darkness, dawn, daylight poems below meditate, first, on the experience of the terrified disciples' in their initial meeting with the risen Christ who comes among them in the locked room (20.19–25). Then comes Thomas' testing encounter with Christ a week later, when Jesus shows him his wounded hands and side (20.26–31). Finally, 'after these things', the exhausted disciples are met by the mysterious man on the shore, who restores their capacity to fish, and feeds them with his own food (21.1–14).

The disciples' darkness (20.19–25)

Night is a locked door,
our chill fears kept safe,
huddled whispers
around the embers of trust.

Dawn is a loosing of your presence,
the peace of your greeting,
light falling from words
like crumbs.

Day is the blow of your heaven breath
coaxing us into flame.

Thomas' darkness (20.26–31)

Night is not having been with the others,
a cold sleet of suspicion
pelting down from the mind's bleak moor.

Dawn, a steady glow of compassion
seeping over the resentful horizon.

Day is sight of your red wounds,
the warmth of your body,
an invitation to touch.

The fishermen's darkness (21.1–14)

Night is floating empty on your teeming sea,
wasted sweat in fruitless labour
spent on depths of dark water.

Dawn is the call of your voice
a deft steer to the catch;
our feet steady on the landing ground
by your fire and food.

Day is a harbour you dig for us,
our kindler, our cook,
our warmth, our welcomer.

Reflecting on the text

John 10.1–10: Jesus, the Good Shepherd

I came that they may have life, and have it abundantly. (John 10.10)

The gatekeeper opens the gate for him, and the sheep hear his
voice. He calls his own sheep by name and leads them out.
When he has brought out all his own, he goes ahead of them,
and the sheep follow him because they know his voice.

(John 10.3–4)

The gift of limitations

In John's Gospel there is a tremendous sense of the wholeness and wonder of life from God and human flourishing. In this reflection on the text I want to look at a dimension of our living that is key to our well-being – the gift (and that is what it is) of limitation and limitations.

I wonder what it is like to be perfect! No fear of failure; the security of knowing that one is right; a doubt-free existence; an ability to function to everyone's satisfaction; energy to be always connected and interested; a tongue that always says the right things. Tenacity and competence to control and overcome whatever comes one's way! How would you define perfection? What would it mean to you?

Whatever the answer, none of us is likely to achieve it. We are limited human beings – splendidly imperfect. Our life is a journey of discovery of our imperfections: of trial and error. In each one there is something to be learned the hard way. It would be nice if there was an easy way of learning!

As we look at the image of the Good Shepherd in this passage let us open up some of the reasons why we battle against our limitations to become invulnerable and then explore that in embracing our imperfections we enlarge the spiritual possibilities of our humanity.

Eric Erikson, a psychologist who has helped us understand much about personal development, is very clear about the crises we face at each stage of life and our need to complete each one successfully if the rest of life is to be satisfyingly healthy. It is through infancy that Erikson has ascribed the task of learning trust. It is in infancy that the capacity for hope is born. The fact that even at the point in our lives when we are weakest our needs are met lays the foundation, he argues, for the notion that whatever our limitations, we will survive. That mothering figures respond to our cries, foresee our needs, tend to our hopelessness, he says, provides the security it takes for human beings to tolerate insecurity.

But the task, however important, is seldom finished in childhood. Mothering figures themselves get sick, go away, become otherwise occupied, and fail to hear us when we cry. And so we carry within ourselves always the possibility that there really is no one out there who will come when we call. No one who cares if we are hurt, no one who will rock our cradle when we cry. The alternative is to take control of the situations ourselves. We must stay alert to the enemy, be defensive, take charge, become a fortress. Mistrust and mastery, power and authority, domination and distance become the name of the game. I live to become sufficient unto myself, in charge of my world, invulnerable. These stances shape our personal and social worlds.

But sooner or later our fortress will fail and fall. The defences come down. The trusses of life begin to quiver. We have glimpses of ourselves as powerless and vulnerable, unsure and open to the elements of life, limited in resources and even more limited in spirit. When we recognize our limitations, then it is possible that they can become our strengths.

The ability to accept the fact that not only are we limited but that limits are the very thing that make us valuable members of the human race comes slowly in life. It is what we need but cannot supply for ourselves that makes us open to the rest of the world. It is what we have that the world needs that gives us any right to be part of the human community at all. The paradox is that to be human is to be imperfect, but it is exactly our imperfection that is our claim to the best of the human condition. We have one another. We are not expected to be self-sufficient. It is precisely our vulnerability that entitles us to love and guarantees us a hearing and a connection from one another – that is what we share in common.

Whose voice, then, do we rely on? Who do we look to and listen to? The definition of success in contemporary society is a tyranny that we all live under. Who do you model yourself on? Who would you really like to be like? What does it mean to be a successful person? Celebrities of every ilk – political, sporting, pop idols or social figures – stand alone, by themselves, under the lights, soaking up the glitter. They are seldom surrounded by the hairdressers, secretaries, agents or consultants who have prepared them to look so good. Superman and Wonder Woman are alive and well in a world that fears vulnerability with a passion. But it is only vulnerability that can prepare us to live well, to understand others, and to take our proper place in the human enterprise.

All of us wrestle with the angels of our inabilities. We posture and evaluate and assess and criticize mercilessly. We insert ourselves into projects we know nothing about. We fail to allow others to love us for our weaknesses as well as for our strengths. Some of us spend time making ourselves imperious, so that there will never be a doubt in anyone's mind who is the god of the day, the messiah of the moment, the king of the mountain, the person in charge, the abbot, the boss, the president, the power. But deep down, that might be the most powerless position of all. If we refuse to ask for help, if we distance ourselves from the strengths of others, if we cling to the myths of authority and power where trust is needed, we leave out a piece of life. We condemn ourselves to ultimate failure because some day, somewhere, we will encounter the thing we cannot do and be confronted with our limitations: our glorious imperfections.

It is trust in the limits of the self that makes us open; it is trust in the gifts of others that makes us secure. We come to realize that we don't have to do everything, that we can't do everything, and that what we can't do is someone else's gift and responsibility. I am a small piece of the cosmic cloak: a necessary piece, but not the only piece. My limitations make space for the gifts of other people. Without the grace of our limitations we would be isolated, dry and insufferable creatures indeed. It is our limitations, and our trust – our dependence on others, and all that springs from them – that save us, deepening our humanity and leading us to God.

So, as we follow the Good Shepherd, let us embrace and befriend our limitations and in doing so allow them to enlarge our spiritual vision.

Action, conversation, questions, prayer

The character of mission: *Knowing, belonging, loving as expressing church.*

Faithful action is the measure of our response to Christ. The challenge facing us is not just to *do* mission but to *be* a people of mission. That is, we are learning to allow every dimension of Church life to be shaped and directed by our identity as a sign, foretaste and instrument of God's reign in Christ.

Action

Name and celebrate the abundant life present in your community at this moment.

Conversation and questions

- How does fear find expression in your discipleship?
- Reflect on the different understandings of Church that belong within your place of worship and community.
- Where do you name Jesus as Lord in your workplace?

Prayer

Life abundant,
God of grace,
you call us by your name
to live without fear.
In peace may we resist
all who kill and despoil your people,
that their hearts might be turned
to the gateway, the Good Shepherd,
our only source of life.
Amen.

7

Pentecost

He breathed on them

Exploring the text

As we have noted on more than one occasion, the equivalent of the Acts account of Pentecost occurs in John's Gospel in 20.19–23. So far in this book we taken the resurrection passages out of order because of the way the Christian year falls. It is now time to turn our attention to this passage. John 20.19–23 is the first of the commissioning resurrection stories (the second being Jesus' forgiveness of Peter, explored in Chapter 6).

One of the key questions for exploring this passage is whether it is, in fact, the same event as Luke records in Acts 2 – the sending of the Holy Spirit. The answer to this must surely be both 'no' and 'yes'. On one level this is an entirely different account. Jesus is still with the disciples. The Holy Spirit does not manifest itself as tongues of fire or as wind (but as Jesus' breath). The disciples, as we saw in the previous chapter, do not go and proclaim the message of Jesus straight away, but return home to Galilee to their fishing boats. On the other hand, Jesus does breathe the Holy Spirit on the disciples and does commission them to forgive and bind sins. It is up to the individual reader to form an opinion as to whether this is the same event told differently, or a different event with similarities.

Whatever your view, some important themes in this story are worth exploring in depth. One of the striking features of

John's Gospel is its themes of relationship and of sending. The Father sent the Son and the Son sent the Spirit. The effect of having Jesus breathe the Spirit on the disciples is that it evokes the image of passing on the baton, from Father to Son to Spirit to disciples. We now follow in Jesus' footsteps in witnessing to the Father because the baton has been passed to us directly from Jesus. When Jesus talks about the Spirit in John 14.26, it is clear that the Spirit (the Advocate or Paraclete there) acts as a mediator not only between God, Jesus and the disciples but between the past and the present as well. The Spirit would act as a means of reminding the disciples of everything that Jesus has said ('the Advocate, the Holy Spirit, whom the Father will send in my name, will teach you everything, and remind you of all that I have said to you': 14.26).

The manner of the sending of the Spirit is also significant, since it recalls a number of passages from the Old Testament. The first and most important passage is, of course, Genesis 2.7 where God breathes into the nostrils of Adam to make him live. Although the Hebrew word for Spirit (*ruah*) is not mentioned in Genesis 2.7, the implication is clear. *Ruah* can be translated either as 'breath' or as 'spirit', and it is the breath of God that makes Adam alive. Similarly in Ezekiel 37, when the dry bones are brought together God declares that he will 'cause breath/spirit (*ruah*) to enter' the body so that it will live. The close connection between breath and spirit make it very difficult to translate this phrase; it could equally mean 'I will cause breath to enter you' or 'I will cause spirit to enter you'. Either way, the point is the same. God breathes his breath/Spirit into the body to give it life. Here in John, Jesus breathes his resurrected breath/Spirit on the disciples to give them life.

We noted above the reference to the Spirit as the Advocate or Paraclete in John 14, and it is worth remembering the import-ance of that description here. If we based our understanding of John's doctrine of the Spirit just from this passage (adding perhaps John 3.1–17 as well), then the Spirit in John would be ephemeral, like breath or wind, and hard to distinguish from the person who receives it. The reference to the Holy Spirit as Paraclete, then, adds a significant counterbalance here. John's use of the word 'Paraclete' to describe the Holy Spirit has occasioned much scholarly discussion. Some argue that it should be understood in terms of the verb *parakaleo*, which means to encourage or to comfort, but it is more likely that John is using the noun as it would have been applied in the legal system of the day, to refer to someone who comes alongside a defendant to speak for them, and be their advocate. This is why many modern translations translate it here as 'Advocate' rather than, as in some older translations, 'Comforter'.

In John, the Advocate intercedes not just for us, but also on behalf of Jesus and his message. John 14.26 points us to the fact that the Advocate's role is to remind the disciples of all Jesus has said. The Spirit then, in John, is not just the breath that animates; it is also the active agent that mediates between the Father and the Son and the disciples, reminding the disciples of Jesus' teaching and what he has sent them to do.

In the context of John 20.19–23 Jesus further elaborates on what he is sending the disciples to do by saying the somewhat surprising words: 'If you forgive the sins of any, they are forgiven them; if you retain the sins of any, they are retained' (John 20.23). This does, however, fit thoroughly into the theme of the rest of the Gospel. In John's Gospel, sin is the refusal to accept the revelation of God in Jesus. Jesus' presence itself brings judgement into the world, since it forces people either to recognize him or not to recognize him. The work of the Spirit in the future will be to continue this dynamic: to bear witness to the one who sent Jesus as well as to who Jesus truly was. The work of the Advocate is to give life to the disciples and to remind them of what Jesus said. The response of people to this message will result in their sin being either forgiven or retained.

Imagining the text

The title of this poem, "*Waiata*," is the Maori word meaning song, chant or psalm, and also the verb 'to sing'. It describes the character of Christian mission, which is celebration and thanksgiving for God's healing action in Christ, for restoring human lives and for the entire created universe. This singing is the gift of the Holy Spirit, a song sung with the breath of Christ himself in many places, languages and cultures. It is a song sung by a missional people who carry it with them as they go, singing God's praise wherever the Spirit takes them. It is a song sung by the created land, sea and sky as God renews the face of the earth.

Waiata (song)

Having been given breath
we grow a forest of voices:
listen how your wind sings through our trees
under many stars.

When you blow, Lord Spirit,
across the vast plains of your realm,
the bush-land of language cries out
in ecstasy and suffering.
Burn in us, your dwelling of cleansed souls;
weave yourself a tent from our dry bones.

Gale-guided
you pull us into fresh harbours
or smash us on the rocks of endeavour.
The work is yours,
the energy is yours,
all is in you
unseen, yet driving.

You teach us the ancient truths in strange places,
uncovering treasure in harsh land
we learn to be poor in the deceitful palaces.
You give us words in dumb prisons.
Exquisite bird, your song calls to us:
hearing your beauty, we too are beautiful.
We welcome all you do,
witnesses of your Witness.

Find roots for the hungry as you go before us,
oils for the sick, leaves for the oppressed;
still us into watching and waiting for your path
as you place its bliss and service
in our hands, on our tongues.

Reflecting on the text

New voices to speak God's love

Hurricanes, tornadoes, earthquakes, volcanic eruptions, tsunami waves – all these fascinate us. Their destructive force seems to come out of nowhere to wreak havoc upon humans and nature. Television gives us the chance to watch the devastation from a safe distance, so that they are merely fantastic images in the mind's eye. A different experience falls to those subjected to these natural forces first hand.

Suddenly comes a new respect for the immense power residing in nature, real and dangerous – a power that before had little meaning or existence, so hidden and remote was it from the predictable routine of daily life. Such an experience changes lives. In an instant the world is turned upside-down by the tremendous release of energy through water, air, fire and earth. An unrecognizable landscape and devastated communities are left in its wake.

Science helps us to understand the systems behind this release of energy. But again and again the world is caught by surprise by its many manifestations. We are continually reminded of our fragile existence within creation.

Another power, a creative power of an altogether different dimension and magnitude, informs our faith. It is this power that changes lives at Pentecost. It is the power that was received by a small, insignificant and unsophisticated group of men and women gathered in Jerusalem waiting for a promise to be fulfilled. The horizons of their world were limited to the countryside of Galilee and Palestine until the Spirit opened their hearts and minds to a greater world beyond.

Nothing could have prepared them for the magnitude of their enlightenment, as they responded to this world-shattering experience of the supernatural creative spirit of God. To stand in its path was to catch fire with divine love. In an instant their world was turned inside-out by a tremendous rush of creative power released into their hearts and minds, souls and bodies, manifesting as flames about their heads.

This inrush of creative energy, which unifies more power-fully than natural powers tear apart, poured itself out among them. The eyes of their hearts were opened to a completely different category of experience, unknown to the world. They saw a new world, through new eyes. The differences of culture and language that separated one person from another crumbled before this unifying power. Suddenly each could speak and hear, with the same understanding, the stories of God's mighty deeds.

As the power of nature opens us up to the enormity of its scale and its ability to destroy, so the power of the Spirit opens our hearts to a new relationship among all people and a new intimacy with God. Man-made bridges crumble before natural disasters; the Spirit builds bridges beyond time and space, between slave and free, man and woman, Jew and Gentile.

It is this power, the power of the Spirit of God, that changes lives at Pentecost. This supernatural power sustains creation, reunites what has been torn apart, reconciles the alienated. The spirit of Pentecost rushes into the world as if out of nowhere, and breathes life into the midst of death. This is Pentecost, the outpouring of God's spirit upon the disciples, then and now.

Then and now, when the spirit rushes in and breaks open old naiveties to reveal the magnitude of God's connecting power, there is no returning to the old frame of reference. Lives are changed for ever: their lives and our lives. Hearts are broken open to a dimension of relationship newly reconciled through the death, resurrection and ascension of the Son to the Father in eternity.

There is no end to the horizon of God's embrace. Disciples see things differently, know things differently, hear things differently, and are sent forth as apostles to share what they see, and know, and hear. God opened the way and taught their hearts; now other languages, other voices, other experiences are no longer foreign to us. All are one in God's love through the power of his reconciling spirit.

For God's power has been received and has revealed the unity of creation, which exceeds our capacity to comprehend, and is beyond the power of nature and humans to destroy. Suddenly the systems of oppression that bind and imprison seem insignificant compared to the marvellous freedom the Spirit of God breathes into humankind, his fragile, beloved children. Now filled with the power of God, we are made capable of extending God's mercy, God's compassion, God's forgiveness to the blind world. For we are made to see through God's eyes that a new covenant has indeed replaced the old, and a people are chosen to deliver the good news: that God calls all into this freedom of his spirit. Year after year on this day, we remember how the first disciples, newly baptized by the Spirit, become apostles and are sent forth, sent out, sent beyond the comfortable yet confining horizons of Galilee. They are sent into the noisy urban world of the diaspora, the pagan world of Rome, where for the first time 'others' – those unlike themselves – will be seen and heard not as alien, suspicious, impure and other, but as 'self': beloved children of God.

We are reminded of the creative energy of God, which overwhelms the destructive powers of humans and nature, so that we too might learn to discern the Spirit as it rushes through our own world, reconciling, reuniting all of creation through us, within us, for us.

The Spirit leads us into a new frame of reference, into the divine dimension of love, where slaves are made children, and where visions and dreams speak of a reality that does not conform to a world dark and bloodied by the violence of our blindness. The Spirit sent forth creates the world anew, if we can but see it.

When the world may seem as if the sun has turned dark and the moon to blood, look about you for men and women going quietly about God's work, creating order out of chaos, offering compassion to the suffering and hope to the desperate. In ordinary and extraordinary ways, at scenes of natural disasters and most unnatural ones, the Spirit of God rushes in to heal and mend, to recreate anew.

There is Pentecost: whenever, in the depths of the most destructive forces of our own hearts, we discover a more creative force compelling us towards reconciliation, towards kindness, towards forgiveness. There the Spirit is rushing in, giving us new eyes to see, new ears to hear, new voices to speak God's love.

Action, conversation, questions, prayer

The character of mission: *Mission as celebration and thanksgiving.*

An important feature of Anglicanism is our belief that worship is central to our common life. But worship is not just something we do alongside our witness to the good news: worship is itself a witness to the world. It is a sign that all of life is holy, that hope and meaning can be found in offering ourselves to God (cf. Romans 12.1).

Action

How might you celebrate the experience of older people in your songs of praise?

Conversation and questions

- What would you most like to change in the pattern of your worship?
- How might we become more open to the guidance of the Holy Spirit?
- Share the reasons why you are thankful to God at the moment.

Prayer

Spirit of truth,
breathe on us and guide us into truth.
Consume the lies
that shroud our world in fear.
Pray in us
with sighs too deep for words
and let all find their voice
to proclaim hope for a new world,
through Jesus Christ our Lord.
Amen.

8

Ordinary Time

―――――•◦•―――――

Exploring the Text

I am the bread of life

Chapter 1 began with an exploration of the great Prologue of John's Gospel. It seems right, therefore, to end the book with an exploration of the other iconic feature of John's Gospel – the 'I am' sayings. Jesus' various 'I am' sayings occur at a number of points throughout the Gospel. To begin with there are the famous 'I am' sayings in which a metaphor makes up the rest of the phrase:

- I am the bread of life (6.35, 48) / which came down from heaven (6.41, 51).
- I am the light of the world (8.12).
- I am the door for the sheep (10.7, 9).
- I am the good shepherd (10.11, 14).
- I am the resurrection and the life (11.25).
- I am the way, the truth and the life (14.6).
- I am the vine (15.1, 5).

These are the classic 'I am' sayings and are the ones that naturally spring to mind when we think of these sayings of Jesus. It is worth noting, however, that Jesus says 'I am' on other occasions too. For example, when he is walking on the Sea of Galilee he says, 'It is I [literally "I am"]; do not be afraid' (6.20); and in conversation with the Jews in 8.58 he says, 'Before Abraham was, I am'.

On one level, it might be tempting to think that these additional 'I am' sayings are of little significance. If someone were to ask, in Greek, 'Is there someone called Mary here?', the response to the question would be 'I am' (in Greek, *ego eimi*). However, in John, it is very rare for anyone but Jesus to use this phrase; and it is more often used in the negative: 'I am not' (see John the Baptist's words at 1.20). This indicates that in John's mind 'I am' are important words for Jesus to say, whether used in a metaphorical phrase or not. When Jesus declares 'I am', whatever form the phrase takes, a meaningful statement is being made.

The importance of the phrase lies in the fact that it is connected to the divine name revealed to Moses in Exodus 3.14. The exchange between God and Moses is significant: when Moses asks God who he should say that he is, God replies, in Hebrew, '*ehyeh asher ehyeh*'. One translation of this is 'I am who I am', but it is interesting to note that the Hebrew verb is imperfect. As a result, it could be translated as either 'I was' or 'I will be'. This makes what God says to Moses even more intriguing, since it could mean 'I was who I was', or 'I will be who I will be', or 'I was who I will be', and so on. In other words, God's being remains constant and will remain constant – past, present and future. Although Greek can't capture this in the way that Hebrew can, it is a theme that is reminiscent of the Prologue of John's Gospel and may have been implied in Jesus' usage of the phrase. It certainly seems implied in statements such as 'Before Abraham was, I am.'

The 'I am' passage that receives the largest use in the lectionary is John 6, which takes up five Sundays in Ordinary Time in Year B. The major challenge of preaching on the passage for these five weeks is to avoid it feeling somewhat repetitive. But its repetition is for good reason. Scholars have argued that the material found in John 6 might well have originated from a synagogue homily, and reflects not only on passages from the Old Testament but also on Jesus' sayings about himself. The argument is that underlying this chapter are two main passages: Exodus 16, with its narrative about God's sending the manna for his people, and Isaiah 54.9—55.6, with a particular emphasis on the start of chapter 55 and the invitation to everyone who thirsts to come to the waters so that they can be satisfied. If this is true, then the passage from Exodus would have been the set Torah (or *seder*) reading for the day, and the passage from Isaiah the *haftarah*, or prophetic accompanying passage.

In Midrashic practice the preacher would weave together the *seder* and the *haftarah*, often using trigger words that allowed them to move backwards and forwards between the two passages, in doing so bringing out the connected meaning of both. In John 6, Jesus' words are also woven in with these two passages and shown to be connected to them. This is why the passage in John feels so repetitive – the repetition is the point. By circling the same idea again and again, Jesus is moving the crowd little by little towards a new understanding of who he is. The key to understanding, and preaching extensively on, this passage is observing the way in which the text circles around Exodus 16, Isaiah 54—55 and Jesus' own sayings, bringing new meaning in each circle.

It is also interesting to notice the language that Jesus uses of himself in this passage. One of the striking features of the metaphorical 'I am' sayings is that after the semi-mystical opening of the phrase, 'I am', the accompanying metaphors are very down to earth – bread, light, door, shepherd and vine. The odd ones out are 'I am the resurrection and the life' and 'I am the way, the truth and the life'; all the other 'I am' sayings compare Jesus to profoundly ordinary artefacts like bread and doors. This is classic John; he loves to place mundane, everyday life next to mind-blowingly profound statements, and by doing so catches the life of humanity into the heart of God.

The language that John uses in chapter 6 is particularly carefully chosen and significant. The discussion about Jesus being the bread of life follows on from the feeding of the 5,000; indeed John makes it clear that those who have been fed by Jesus are the same people who then converse with him about bread. What is hard to convey in English is that two different words for 'bread' are used here. The 'bread' that Jesus gives to the crowd indicates a very poor-quality barley loaf which was hard to chew or digest. The word for 'bread' that Jesus uses to describe himself translates as bread of the finest kind, made of high-quality wheat. Not only will this bread last for ever, it is also of a far higher quality than the bread they received at the feeding of the 5,000.

This lends significance to Jesus' discourse – if the crowd are prepared to go to such great lengths to get basic barley bread, which wore down their teeth and sat heavy in the stomach, what will they be prepared to do to receive the never-ending, finest-quality sustenance offered by Jesus?

Imagining the text

These simple verses offer a meditation on Jesus the bread of life (John 6). Jesus is the bread who gives his energy and sustenance to anxious, hungry disciples: when they are feeding searching people in their thousands (6.1–14), and in a more intimate way after the resurrection (John 21); he is the one who not only comes to them with reassurance in the storm but gets into the vulnerable boat alongside them (6.16–21); he is the teacher who listens to persistent questions and opens them up into a feast of new understanding (6.25–27, 28–29); he is the one who feeds the hungry world with signs of God's true purposes of love, ultimately through his own self-giving on the cross (6.30–34); he is the one who feeds them spiritually through his word and in the Eucharist, drawing them into the eternal life of God in which he too shares.

Food for the journey

From the anxious hunger
fish and bread
feed him to us.

Out on fearful waters
a companion
rowing alongside us.

In the crowded questions
fresh space
he opens up for us.

To our search for meaning
the signs
why we may trust him.

For uncertain futures
his eternal present
abiding with us.

Reflecting on the text

I am the living bread: John 6.35, 41–51

Imagine the scene. It must have been an amazing sight: thousands gathered, listening, learning, and – all of a sudden – hungry. The disciples are asked to 'care for those gathered', and all that they can come up with is a little boy with five loaves and two fish. Jesus takes, gives thanks, and begins to feed those who are gathered there. Jesus provides for them beyond belief.

However (like many things in John's Gospel) not everything is what it seems. What are these people really hungry for? What are they looking for? The 'Word made flesh' – one who shows us the Father, one who connects us and makes us participants of the divine life.

It is not uncommon for us to confuse the thing with the person, the symptom for the problem, the want for the need. Those that are fed that day now come looking for more; Jesus faces them with the reality of his identity, with the opportunity for a different life, if they 'choose' to participate in it. Those of us who claim Christ as our Lord find ourselves being fed by Christ's own presence, and it is in that feeding that we are participants in the divine life. God reaching out to us, providing a way for grace, opening the doors for the holy to live among us: again and again and again.

In our eating and our drinking we too participate in this long story of a God who 'feeds' and a people who serve; we share in a God who gives of God's self and a people who follow in the way. No wonder those of us who share in the eating of the bread of life are participating in something more!

This text might invite us to dig a little deeper. We might warn ourselves that those of us who eat this bread eat it at our peril:

We cannot eat of this bread and forget.

We cannot eat of this bread and walk away.

We cannot eat of this bread and go on with life as usual.

In fact, when we eat and drink, when we become part of the central activity and posture of our life together, the central reason for our gathering – we too are saying that God's will for all of us, and all the world, is to be restored, saved, healed, made whole!

We are called to be part of a new reality and to draw others into this. It is life-changing, as we are transformed into God's own. When we eat and drink together, we recognize that Jesus, the 'bread of life', is showing us the way to a life that is available and yet mysterious, showing us that we too have access to the divine life, that we too can come into God's presence.

We reflect on this in what has been a testing time economically for many people in the UK. Some churches have opened food banks offering support to those who are deprived. This has come out of the vision of the churches to 'feed Christ's sheep'. Challenged by this, we might ask: what would it look like for us to be a Church that feeds people? How would we feed them?

In our eating and our drinking, in our sharing of our resources, we have the opportunity to make sure that those resources we offer, the table that we spread, the door that we open, become part and parcel of God's activity in the world. People – everyday people, hungry people, needy people, people in desperate need of relationship, in desperate need of one another – can begin to experience the 'wonder-full' healing and restorative power of Jesus.

Maybe if we spent more time and attention in becoming a 'feeding people', if we put our attention in becoming a community of the 'bread of life', if we took more seriously the reality of God's own presence in our meal, we would spend less time and attention on things that separate us, that exclude others, that close our doors, and that question God's image in others.

Eating assumes that we are hungry, that we are in need of sustenance. Part of the challenge of the Christian life is the recognition of our dependence and our interdependence. We need to see that in eating we are recognizing our own dependence on God: no longer relying on signs and wonders and instead being aware of our own need. We need to see that in this eating and drinking, in this gathering, we are able to experience God's self: we who are in need of sustenance, in need of something more, truly seeing God.

Part of the challenge is to recognize that there are many around us who go about each day, every day, without the sustenance they need. As we gather for feasting day after day, week after week, many have no such sustenance.

'I am the living bread!' says Jesus . . . Open your eyes! See the light!

Maybe now we can recognize that we too – *we too*, you and I – have been beneficiaries of an amazing life. We have found our sustenance and instead of using it to propel us into the neediness and hunger of the world, instead of using that sustenance to energize us into speaking on behalf of those that have no voice, instead of allowing that sustenance to call us to task, again and again, about the ways in which our own life is part of the problem, we have continued eating our fill, acting as if we've earned it, ignoring the plight of those who need this sustenance the most.

The community called the Church is at its core a community of people who hunger. We are a community of people called together around a table, whose identity is rooted in what it means to be sustained by the presence of Christ's self each and every time we gather together.

From the very beginning of the story of faith, God has been giving us of God's self and inviting us to take this sustenance and use it to be a source of light to the world on behalf of God's kingdom. So part of our sacrifice of praise and thanksgiving is our recognition that when we leave our churches and end our gatherings of prayer and praise, we are to walk out of the doors and work tirelessly for the sustenance and feeding of a hungry, hungry world.

May our congregations, may our gatherings, may our conversations, become the centre – the active centre – of creating this future, of creating eschatological reality. May we together begin, in our eating, to make a way to the Father. May we become a people that begin to extend life eternal to a hungry world, a people who live out the meaning of sharing in the life of Jesus.

May we become the body that feeds them; may we become the body that proclaims the identity of the bread of life to this broken and hungry world.

Action, conversation, questions, prayer

The character of mission: *Mission in context.*

Mission is always responsive to the setting in which the gospel is being proclaimed and lived out, so mission is expressed in many different ways – we could say *incarnated* in different cultures and situations.

Action

Consider the context within which you are a Christian disciple.
How might your church feed the people?

Conversation and questions

- How might you enliven the way in which your church celebrates
  the harvest?
- What does spiritual hunger mean for you?
- Are there opportunities to draw people into the worshipping
  community through celebrating events involving the sharing
  of food?

Prayer

Unseen God,
drawing all people
to the end of our desires,
teach us to know
true bread from false
and to feed on him
who shares our flesh,
to share your love,
Jesus Christ, our communion.
Amen.

Further reading and resources

The classic commentary on John remains Raymond Brown, *The Gospel According to John* (two volumes, New York: Doubleday, 1998). It is now out of print and can be hard to find. There is, however, a shorter version which covers the epistles as well: *The Gospel and Epistles of John* (Collegeville, MN: Liturgical Press, 1992).

Other more modern commentaries include Andrew Lincoln, *The Gospel According to John* (Ada, MI: Baker Academic, 2013); Francis J. Moloney, *The Gospel of John* (Sacra Pagina, Collegeville, MN: Liturgical Press, 2005); Jerome Neyrey, *The Gospel of John* (Cambridge: Cambridge University Press, 2006).

There are a number of introductions to the book. The two best are: Ruth Edwards, *Discovering John* (London: SPCK, 2014) and Jan Van Der Watt, *An Introduction to the Johannine Gospel and Letters* (London: T&T Clark, 2008).

Richard Bauckham, *The Testimony of the Beloved Disciple: Narrative, History, and Theology in the Gospel of John* (Ada, MI: Baker Academic, 2007) is an excellent and thought-provoking longer book on John's Gospel.

For a profound meditation on John by the founder of the L'Arche Community, see Jean Vanier, *Drawn into the Mystery of Jesus through the Gospel of John* (London: Darton, Longman and Todd, 2004).

Archbishop William Temple's reflections, *Readings in St John's Gospel* (1945) also yield valuable insights.

See more about the five marks of mission at: <www.anglicancommunion. org/ministry/mission/fivemarks.cfm#sthash.OHoBdWZL.dpuf>.

James Woodward is a Canon of Windsor. He has written extensively in the area of pastoral and practical theology. His recent publications include Valuing Age: Pastoral Ministry with Older People (SPCK, 2008). He is particularly interested in how Christian discipleship nurtures and deepens human well-being. For further information about his work, see his website <www.jameswoodward.info>.

Paula Gooder is Theologian in Residence for the Bible Society, and a freelance writer and lecturer in biblical studies. Her recent publications include Searching for Meaning: An Introduction to Interpreting the New Testament (2008), Heaven (2011) and, with Michael Perham, Echoing the Word (2013), all published by SPCK.

Mark Pryce is Bishop's Adviser for Clergy Continuing Ministerial Education in the Diocese of Birmingham, and an honorary Canon of Birmingham Cathedral. His other publications include the Literary Companion to the Lectionary (2001) and the Literary Companion for Festivals: Readings for Commemorations Throughout the Year (2003), both published by SPCK.

CPSIA information can be obtained at www.ICGtesting.com
Printed in the USA
LVOW11s0345090316

478342LV00001B/24/P